CAMBRIDGE

Official Cambridge Exam Preparation

Be Curious

Pupil's Book 4

Caroline Nixon | Michael Tomlinson

Map of the book

	Vocabulary	Grammar	Cross-curricular	Literature	Assessment
Welcome to Diversicus Page 4	Main character names Greetings and introductions	**Language review** Questions and answers Greetings			
1 Practice time Mission: Plan a week in the life of a circus artist Page 6	Telling the time Activity verbs **Sounds and spelling:** numbers	**Review: question words** *how, what, when, where, which, who, why* ***was/were + could*** *I could hop on one leg when I was four.* *I couldn't skip.*	***Balancing act*** Learn about balance and coordination A Russian Olympic athlete	***The circus child*** A real-life story Social and emotional skill: perseverance	A1 Movers Reading and Writing Part 6
2 What's for breakfast? Mission: Become a restaurant owner Page 18	Food and drink Past simple irregular verbs **Sounds and spelling:** *c* spelling for 's' and 'k' sound	**Defining relative clauses** *It's the place where I studied.* *Can you see the woman who is cooking in the kitchen?* *They're the mountains which I climbed with my father.* **Past simple + *with/when*** *When we finished lunch we went to the funfair.*	***Food, glorious food*** Learn about food and nutrition Breakfast in China and around the world	***The old man and the small fish*** A real-life story Social and emotional skill: showing respect for decisions of others	A1 Movers Listening Part 5
3 A healthy body Mission: Become a health expert Page 30	Parts of the body Health problems **Sounds and spelling:** *kn* and *n* spelling for 'n' sound	**Review of comparative and superlative adjectives, *as … as*** *I'm not as strong as you.* *Jenny is taller than you.* *Ivan is the strongest man here.* ***want/need* + infinitive** *I want to go to the party.* *You need to drink.* *I don't want to drink.*	***Work your body*** Learn about bones and joints Yoga in Indonesia	***Too-too-moo and the Komodo dragon*** A fantasy play script Social and emotional skill: showing empathy for others	A1 Movers Reading and Writing Part 4
	Review Units 1–3				
4 Fun in the jungle Mission: Create a jungle adventure park Page 44	Natural features Past simple verbs **Sounds and spelling:** *l, ll* and *le* spelling for 'l' sound	**Adverbs** *well, badly, loudly, quietly, quickly, slowly, carefully, beautifully, hard, fast* **Comparative adverbs** *Elephants can move faster than snakes.* *Monkeys can climb better than tigers.* *Bears can run more quickly than monkeys.*	***From the roots to the flower*** Learn about plants and how they grow Carnivorous plants in India and around the world	***The story of Rama and Sita*** An Indian myth Social and emotional skill: helping others	A1 Movers Reading and Writing Part 5

Welcome to Diversicus

1 0.02 **Listen. What is Diversicus?**

The Friendly family are going on tour with Diversicus. Today is their first day.

2 0.03 **Who says it? Say the name.**

3 **Play the game. Ask and answer.**

Who's got purple hair? — Rose.

What's the name of the circus? — Diversicus.

DIVERSICUS

0.04

4 **Act out the story.**

1 Practice time

1 **Watch the video. Ask and answer.**

What are your hobbies?
Do you practise your hobbies every day?

mission Plan a week in the life of a circus artist

In this unit I will:

1. Prepare a weekly schedule.
2. Add practice time to the schedule.
3. Add a warm-up activity to the schedule.
- ★ Present a schedule to the class.

1 1.01 Listen. Then say the letter.

Diversicus is in Russia. This morning, Mr Friendly and Rose are talking about meals and meal times.

a half past twelve

b midnight

c half past eight

d half past nine

e seven o'clock

f half past six

g eight o'clock

h midday

2 What time is it? Ask and answer.

What time is it? It's half past twelve.

3 Ask and answer.

breakfast a snack lunch dinner wake up go to bed

What time do you have breakfast? I have breakfast at half past seven.

Be Curious about Russia

Russia is the biggest country in the world and it's on two continents: Asia and Europe. You can celebrate New Year's Eve 11 times in Russia. Why? Because it has 11 time zones!

DIVERSICUS

1.02

1 1.03 **Listen and say *yes* or *no*.**

1 **Describe the picture. What are they doing?**

2 **Read. Answer the questions.**

Diversicus is a circus. There are acrobats and clowns, but there aren't any animals. The acrobats get up at half past six and they have breakfast early because they start practising at nine o'clock. Acrobats have to climb, run and jump. The strong acrobats catch the others in the air. It's very exciting. Their job is beautiful, but it's dangerous, too.

1. What is Diversicus?
2. What time do the acrobats get up?
3. Why do they have breakfast early?
4. What time do they start practising?
5. Which acrobats catch the others in the air?

Grammar spotlight

1.04

Which country are we in?	We're in **Russia**.
Why are you running?	**Because** school starts in ten minutes.
What time do they have lunch?	They have lunch at **half past twelve**.

3 **Imagine you meet an acrobat from Diversicus. What do you want to know about him/her? Write three questions.**

mission STAGE 1

Prepare your schedule.

- Choose which circus artist you'd like to be.
- Work with a partner.
- Ask and answer to complete your partner's weekly schedule.

What time do you have breakfast?

I have breakfast at eight o'clock.

What time do you go to bed on Mondays?

At nine o'clock.

My mission diary

Activity Book page 6

1 Listen and do the actions. Then sing the song. 1.05

Hop, skip and dance, climb, climb, climb.
Jump to your places, it's practice time.

Dress up, dress up. Put your costumes on.
We haven't got time, we haven't got long.

Hello, kids! Are you in or out?
You must be quiet, you mustn't shout!

Ivan, don't laugh. Stand in your place.
You must catch Marc with a smile on your face.

Marc, catch Lily! Hold her legs!
She mustn't fall into the net.

Chorus

2 Describe the picture in Activity 1 to a partner. Use the words in the picture.

The people in purple clothes are dancing.

Let's talk about parties. Do you like dressing up for parties? What clothes do you wear?

3 Write three sentences about the picture.

Two acrobats are dressing up.

1 1.07 **Listen and match Daisy and Peter to a picture.**

Daisy

Peter

a

b

c

Grammar spotlight 1.08

I **could hop** on one leg when I **was** four.

I **couldn't skip**.

2 **Think about when you were four. Write three sentences about what you could and couldn't do.**

3 **Ask and answer.**

ride a bike swim climb trees play the guitar ride a skateboard skate sing dance hop skip cook

Could you ride a bike when you were three?

No, I couldn't.

mission STAGE 2

Add a practice time to the schedule.

- Ask your partner about when they practise.
- Add this information to their weekly schedule.

When do you do practise?

I practise on Tuesdays at five o'clock. I jump and skip.

My mission diary

Activity Book page 6

Balancing act

1 Watch the video.

2 1.09 Listen and read. Answer the question.

Can you ride a bike? Do you like ice skating or doing gymnastics? When you do these activities what helps you not to fall all the time? It's your sense of balance. Your brain controls your sense of balance. The brain is a very complicated organ. Different parts control different things. The cerebellum is the part of the brain that controls balance. Without this, it would be difficult to walk or even stand up.

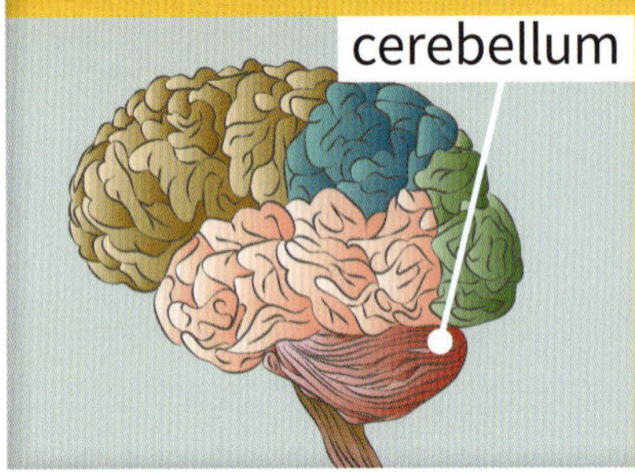

Which other activities need a sense of balance?

3 Look at the pictures. Which activities need balance?

1 

2 

3 

4 

4 Read and try the activities.

Test your balance. Try these activities.

Tightrope walking.

Place a long piece of string on the floor in a straight line. Walk along the string to the end. Try it with your eyes closed, or try going backwards!

Who's the tallest?

Work with a partner. Put one paper plate at a time onto your partner's head. Who can keep the most paper plates on their head?

5 1.10 **Listen and read the text about a Russian athlete. Answer the question.**

What new move did Olga Korbut perform in 1972?

Olga Korbut

One sport that needs a really good sense of balance is gymnastics. And who is the queen of balance? Russian Olympic gymnast, Olga Korbut!

Olga Korbut was born in 1955 in Grodno. At the time Grodno was part of the USSR (the Soviet Union).

She studied in a school that had a special programme for sports people. She began to train for the Olympic team.

At the Olympic Games in 1972, Olga was 17 years old and the youngest member of the team. She was also very small, only 1.5 metres tall, but she was very strong. Her routines were fast and exciting and she was everyone's favourite gymnast.

Olga Korbut won four gold medals and two silver medals for the USSR in the 1972 and 1976 Olympics. In 1972, she performed new moves including the Korbut Flip. They don't do this move in competitions now because people think it is too dangerous!

It is still exciting to watch Olga Korbut's routines, but don't forget that she had to train for many hours every day to become a top gymnast. Would you like to be a gymnast?

6 **Read the text again. Complete the mind map.**

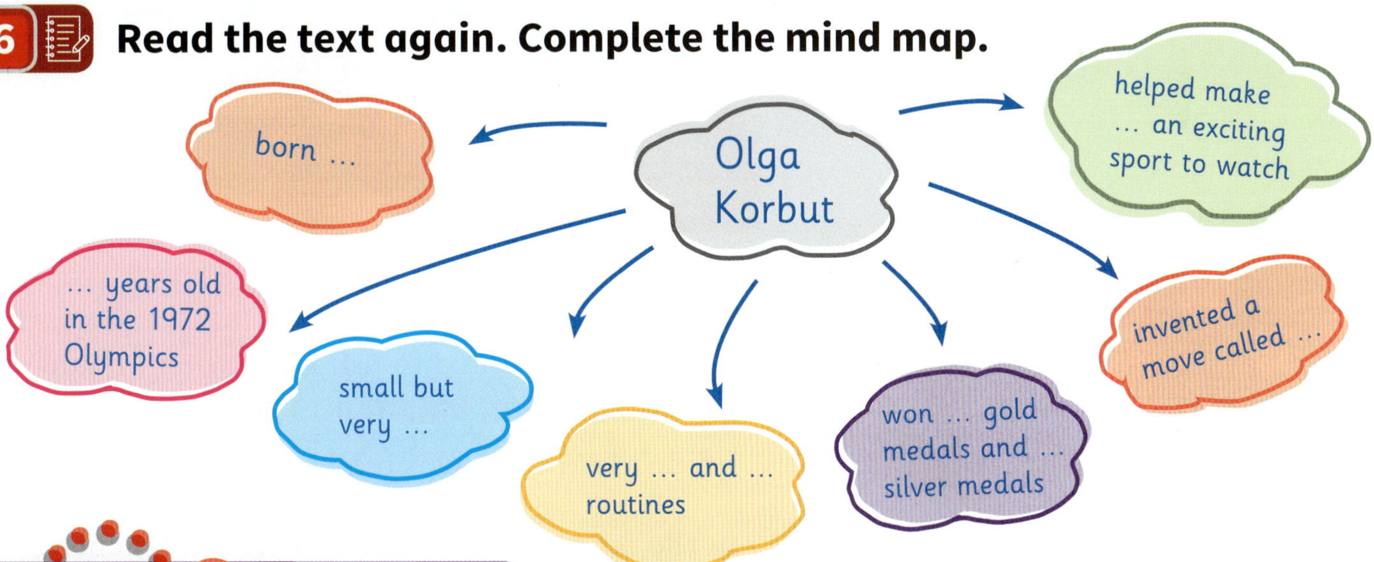

mission STAGE 3

Add a warm-up routine to your schedule.

- Work in groups.
- Think of a warm-up activity to do for your practice.
- Decide where to put it in your schedule.

My mission diary
Activity Book page 6

1 Look at the pictures. Answer the questions.

1 Would you like to be part of a circus? Why? Why not?

2 How old do you think the girl in the circus is?

1.11 THE CIRCUS CHILD

Can you imagine being in a circus? Travelling all over the world, playing with clowns, flying through the air on a trapeze, or jumping on trampolines all day? No? Well, let me tell you about it.

My name is Anastasia. I was born in the circus. My parents are Russian acrobats with *Captain Adventure's Travelling Circus* and my dream was always to be just like them and perform on stage.

Every day I wanted to ask Dad when I could go on stage with him. But I was afraid to. I didn't know if I was ready.

In the mornings I had classes with a teacher online. They started at nine o'clock. My parents said I had to do well at school. In the afternoons I practised acrobatics with my dad for hours. We practised until dinner at half past seven.

My dad helped me improve and learn new moves. 'Let's try a backflip,' he said one day, ready to catch me if I fell. I couldn't do backflips then, but I can now.

'Great! Again! Fantastic! Again!' he told me. I practised a lot. I really wanted to do it.

After training, my friend Yuri usually came over to give me support.
'Soon,' he always said, and hugged me.

I practised really hard every day for years, then last month it finally happened. Dad said, 'I think you are ready to go on stage now. How about Saturday?'
'Really?' I shouted and jumped up and down.

Immediately, I ran to tell Yuri the good news. 'I told you!' he laughed. 'You practised a lot, and practice makes perfect.'

And that was how my dream came true. Now I perform in the circus every week.

2 Answer the questions.

1. What does Anastasia do every day? Why does she do this?
2. How did Anastasia feel at the beginning of the story? How does she feel now?
3. What do you practise every day? Why?

1 Talk about the picture and point.

She's got a black hat.

He's riding a bike.

2 Look at the picture and choose the correct word.

1 The clown with the toy plane is ***walking*** / ***skipping*** / ***dancing***.

2 One hat is black and one hat is ***yellow*** / ***pink*** / ***green***.

3 One of the children has got a ***kitten*** / ***rabbit*** / ***penguin***.

3 Look at the picture and complete the sentences.

1 What is the boy doing? He's …

2 The small clown is …

3 The man in the white shirt is …

Write 2 different sentences about the picture.

4 Say two more things about the picture.

I like this circus.

The clowns are funny.

mission in action!

Present a schedule to the class.

My mission diary
Activity Book page 6

- In your groups, choose a schedule.
- Present the schedule to the class.

This is our schedule. On weekdays, we wake up at eight o'clock. We study at ten o'clock. We do our warm-up at three o'clock. We practise jumping at five o'clock.

- Perform your warm-up activity.

Can you remember?

1 What time do the circus artists have breakfast on Mondays?
2 Who is Marc?
3 Why does Ivan eat a lot?
4 What couldn't Peter do when he was four?
5 Name three activities that need a sense of balance.
6 What couldn't Anastasia do that she can do now?

2 What's for breakfast?

1 **Watch the video. Ask and answer.**

What time do you usually eat breakfast?
What do you usually eat?

mission Become a restaurant owner

In this unit I will:

1. Create a restaurant.
2. Talk about restaurants with a partner.
3. Create a restaurant menu.
★ Write a review about a restaurant.

1 2.01 Listen. What do Rose and Ivan like for breakfast?

Diversicus is in China. Today, Mr Friendly, Ivan and the children are in the supermarket, shopping for food.

2 2.02 Say the chant.

3 Match. Then offer your partner food and drink.

milk noodles water soup coffee
lemonade pasta tea salad rice

1	a glass of	a	coffee
2	a cup of	b	chocolate sauce
3	a bottle of	c	cereal
4	a bowl of	d	milkshake

Would you like a glass of milk?

Yes, please.

Be Curious about China

The Chinese probably invented the world's first ice cream - more than 2200 years ago! They mixed rice and milk then put it under the snow.

DIVERSICUS

2.03

1 2.04 **Listen. Who says it?**

1 **Describe the picture. What are they doing?**

2 **Read and check. Choose the words to complete the text.**

Look at these children [1]who are climbing up the mountain. They're on the Great Wall of China. It's a wall [2]... people built many years ago. It's famous because it's the [3]... wall in the world. The Great Wall is a beautiful place [4]... people enjoy walking and [5]... photos. Would you like to [6]... on the Great Wall?

1	who	which	where
2	who	which	where
3	longest	fastest	smallest
4	who	which	where
5	doing	making	taking
6	walk	walked	walking

2.05 Grammar spotlight

It's the place **where** I studied.

Can you see the woman **who** is cooking in the kitchen?

They're the mountains **which** I climbed with my father.

3 **Play the guessing game.**

It's the thing which we use to take photos.

A camera.

mission STAGE 1

Create a restaurant.

- Choose a name and a description for your restaurant.
- Prepare a restaurant sign.
- In groups, talk about your restaurants.

My restaurant's called *Happy Noodle*. It's a Chinese restaurant where you can eat noodles for breakfast.

My mission diary

Activity Book page 18

1 2.06 **Listen and match the words to the pictures. Then sing the song.**

Yesterday we **drove** to town.
We saw the place where May grew up.
She told us all about her school,
And the teacher who taught her there.

Oh, we **got dressed up**.
Oh, we had a great day.
Oh, we **wrote** this song.
Oh, we took some photos of it all.

Yesterday we saw May's sister.
She **gave** us all a bowl of noodles.
After lunch we **climbed** the Great Wall,
Which they built years before.

Oh, we got dressed up.
Oh, we had a great day.
Oh, we wrote this song.
Oh, we took some photos.

Oh, we got dressed up.
Oh, we had a great day.
Oh, we wrote this song.
Oh, we took some photos of it all.
We had a great day.

2 **Find the past simple form of these verbs in the song.**

see write tell build take drive teach give have grow get climb

3 **Ask and answer about the song.**

Did they drive to the beach?

No, they didn't. They drove to the town.

Did they see the place where May grew up?

Yes, they did.

What did you do yesterday afternoon?

1 2.08 **Listen. What did Jack like best?**

a

b

c

Grammar spotlight

2.09

When we **finished** lunch we **went** to the funfair.

When the bus **arrived** we all **got** on it.

We **were** sad **when** the bus **came** to take us home.

2 **Ask and answer.**

Questions: arrive at school | finish school | get home from school | finish breakfast/lunch/dinner | finish your homework

Answers: play | study | watch TV | go to school | do my homework | read | clean my teeth | listen to music

What did you do when you finished breakfast yesterday?

When I finished breakfast yesterday, I cleaned my teeth.

3 **What did you do yesterday? Write three sentences with *when*.**

mission STAGE 2

Talk about restaurants with a partner.

- Talk about restaurants that you like and why you like them with a partner.

When my family and I went to Mallorca, we went to a restaurant by the sea. I'd like my restaurant to be near the sea.

My mission diary

Activity Book page 18

Food, glorious food

1 **Watch the video.**

2 2.10 **Listen and read. What are the five main food groups?**

We know that we need food to stay alive, and that it can be delicious! But we also know that we need to eat different types of food and the right amounts to stay healthy. There are five main food groups:

3 **Match these foods to the groups in Activity 2.**

a

b

c

d

e

4 **Think of two breakfast foods for each food group.**

Carbohydrates and fibre – cereal and ...

5 **How healthy are your breakfast foods in Activity 4? Give each a score out of five.**

1 = very unhealthy
5 = very healthy

I think that cereal is 3. It's sometimes healthy and sometimes unhealthy when it's got a lot of sugar.

6 2.11 Look at the breakfasts. Where do you think they are from? Listen and check.

1

2

3

4

7 2.12 Listen and read. Where is this breakfast from?

People often have breakfast at around seven o'clock in China because children usually go to school before eight o'clock. People often buy breakfast from a street stall and they eat it as they travel to work or school. China is a very large country and the breakfasts are different in different cities. The most popular breakfast is soya milk with youtiao. Youtiao are like long fried doughnuts. People dip them into the soya milk. Other people prefer rice noodles or buns with meat.

8 Talk to a partner about your breakfast.

I usually have ... for breakfast.

My favourite breakfast is ...

mission STAGE 3

Create a restaurant menu.

- Think of some healthy food to include in your menu.
- Create and design your menu.

My mission diary
Activity Book page 18

1 **Look at the pictures. Describe the people in the story.**

2.13 The old man and the small fish

My name is Ching-Yun. I am an old man. I live in a village near the Huangshan Mountain. My granddaughter calls me 'The Happiest Man in China'.

Every day my granddaughter comes to visit me before she goes to school. Her name is Wen. She is eight years old. Wen makes breakfast for me. I have the same thing every morning – noodles and a cup of green tea. After breakfast, I tell Wen the old stories my grandpa told me when I was a boy.

It was cold that morning. Wen arrived early.
'Yéye,' she said, 'do you want something different for breakfast today – perhaps some rice or some bread?'
I said, 'No, thank you, Wen. I'm very happy with my noodles and my tea.'
'Why do you have the same thing for breakfast every day, Yéye?' Wen asked me.
I finished my breakfast and then I told Wen the story of 'The small fish which swam in the same part of the lake'.

2

There was once a small fish, and every day the small fish swam in the same part of the lake. Its friends didn't understand. They said, 'Come with us to a new part of the lake, small fish.'
But the small fish said, 'No, thank you. I'm happy here.'

One morning, the friends of the small fish didn't go to a new part of the lake.
'Why didn't you swim to a new part of the lake today?' said the small fish.

'We know every part of the lake now,' the friends of the small fish said, happily. 'But this part is still the best, so we're staying here with you.'

The next morning, Wen made me noodles and green tea. This time, she didn't ask me if I wanted something different for my breakfast.

2 Read and discuss with a partner. Are your answers the same or different?

1 Why do you think Wen's grandfather doesn't want to change what he has for breakfast?

2 Do you think it's better to always do the same thing (like Wen's grandfather) or always try something different? Why?

1 2.14 **Listen. Are the pictures correct? Say *yes* or *no*.**

2 2.15 **Look at the picture in Activity 3. Listen and finish the sentences.**

The woman is between the cupboard and the man.

3 2.16 **Listen and find the things to colour and the place to write the word. There is one example.**

Listen carefully for prepositions and write the word in the correct place!

mission in action!

Write a review about a restaurant.

My mission diary
Activity Book page 18

- Talk to a friend about the restaurant which you went to.

Which restaurant did you go to?

I went to the Chinese restaurant. It was great!

- Write a review about the restaurant.

This restaurant was good because …
I really liked …
I didn't like … as much because …

Can you remember?

1. What's the man in the supermarket in China making?
2. Which places did May take Ivan and the children to see when they went to her town?
3. What did Jim, Jenny and their friends do after lunch?
4. Name three food items in the food group 'dairy'.
5. Where do people eat 'youtiao' for breakfast?
6. What did Wen's grandfather always have for breakfast?

3 A healthy body

1 Watch the video. Ask and answer.

What do you do to stay healthy?

Why's it important to exercise and eat healthily?

mission Become a health expert

In this unit I will:

1. Create a health plan.
2. Visit the doctor.
3. Add some healing tips to my health plan.
- Make a health advice poster.

1 3.01 Listen. How did Ivan cut his finger?

Diversicus is in Indonesia. This morning Ivan is doing exercise on the beach. The children are watching him.

2 3.02 Say the chant.

3 3.03 Listen and say *yes* or *no*.

4 Write two sentences about the picture.

Be Curious about Indonesia

The biggest lizards in the world live in Indonesia. They're called Komodo dragons. They weigh about 75kg, but they can eat over 60kg of food in one meal! That's a very big breakfast!

1 3.05 **Listen and say the number.**

1 Look at the picture. Which part of their body do you think is the strongest?

2 Choose the words to complete the text.

A human tower is one of the [1]*exciting* / *most exciting* things to see, but it's one of the [2]*most* / *more* dangerous, too. Look at these three people. The person at the bottom has to be the [3]***stronger*** / ***strongest***. The person in the middle isn't as [4]***biggest*** / ***big*** as the person at the bottom, but she's [5]***stronger*** / ***strong*** than the person at the top. The person at the top is [6]***small*** / ***smaller*** and [7]***thinner*** / ***thinnest*** than the other two people. Her job isn't [8]***easier*** / ***easy*** than theirs; it's as difficult [9]***as*** / ***than*** theirs and sometimes it's [10]***more*** / ***most*** dangerous. Would you like to try it?

Grammar spotlight

3.06

I'm not **as** strong **as** you.	Jenny is **taller than** you.	Ivan is **the strongest** man here.

3 Make sentences about your family. Use these words.

tall strong big clever funny careful boring interesting loud quiet

My grandma isn't as tall as my dad.

My sister's funnier than my brother.

I'm the loudest person in my family.

mission STAGE 1

Create a health plan.

- Work with a partner. Choose three parts of the body.
- Think of ways to keep these parts of the body healthy and fit.
- Add these ideas to your health plan.

My mission diary

Activity Book page 30

1 3.07 Listen and match the names to the words. Then sing the song.

They're all sick,
They're all ill.
They're all ill,
They're all sick.
Doctor, Doctor,
Please be quick!

What's the problem?
What's the matter?
What's the problem?
What's the matter?

He's got a **cough**
And a **temperature**,
She's got a **sore throat**
And a **cold**.

Chorus

My back hurts.
I've got a **backache**.
My stomach hurts.
Ooh **stomach-ache**.

Chorus

2 Play the guessing game. Ask and answer.

Does your head hurt? — No, it doesn't.

Does your back hurt? — Yes, it does.

You've got backache. — Yes, that's right.

3 3.09 Listen. Write the words.

1 3.10 **Listen. What does Vicky need to do?**

Grammar spotlight 3.11

I **want to go** to the party.
You **need to drink**.
I **don't want to drink**.

2 **Write questions and answers with *but*.**

sing | eat some cake | play football | go to a party | play the guitar | study

a stomach-ache | a sore throat | ill | fingers hurt | a headache | a temperature

> What's the matter?
> I want to play football after school, but I've got a headache.
> You need to sit down, but you can watch the game.

3 **What do you want to do? What do you need to do? Write two sentences for each question.**

> I want to go to the cinema. I need to do my homework.

mission STAGE 2

Visit the doctor.

- Work with a partner. One person is a doctor and the other person is a patient.
- Patient: Tell the doctor what's wrong with you.
- Doctor: Give the patient some advice.

What's the matter?

I want to go to the football match, but I've got a temperature.

You need to stay at home and rest.

- Swap roles. Then add the advice to your health plan.

My mission diary
Activity Book page 30

Work your body

1 Watch the video. Then read the text.

Did you know there are over 200 bones in our bodies? Bones shape our body and hold us together. Between each bone we have a joint. Joints help us to move. It's important to protect our bones and joints, especially when we're doing sports and other dangerous activities.

2 Match the parts of the body to the bones and joints.

1 
shoulder

2 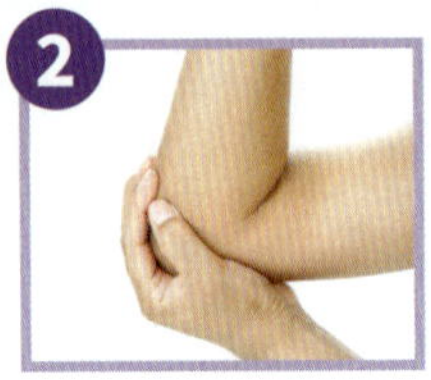
elbow

3 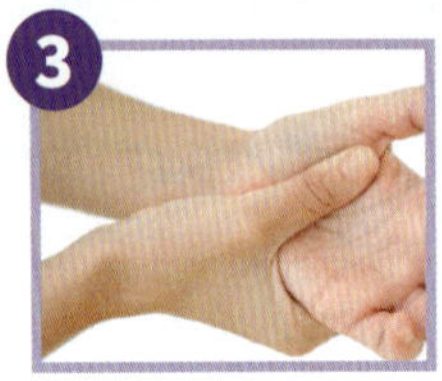
wrist

4 
hip

5 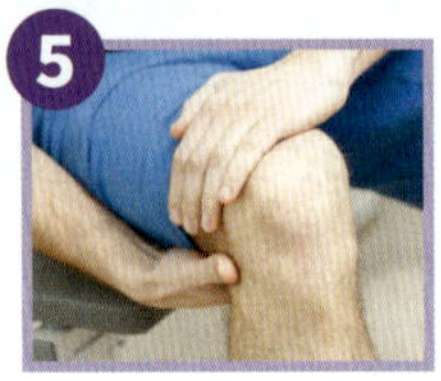
knee

6 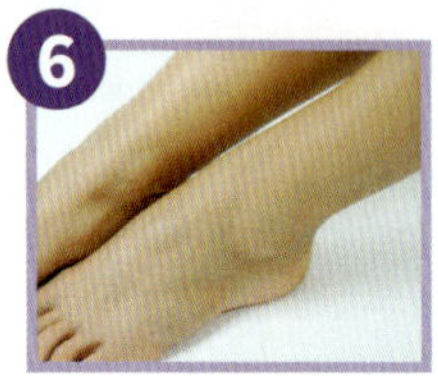
ankle

a 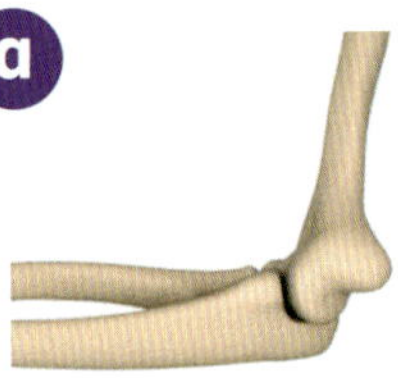

b 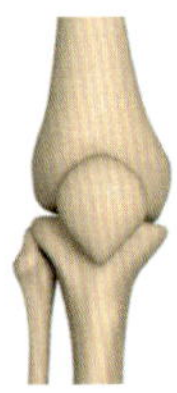

c 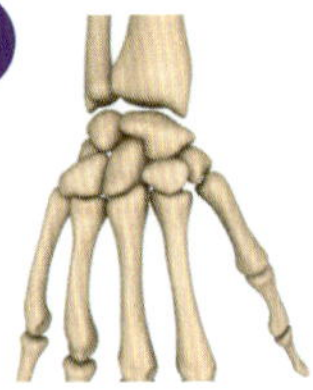

d 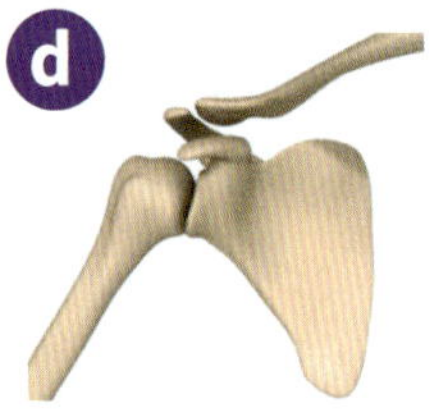

e 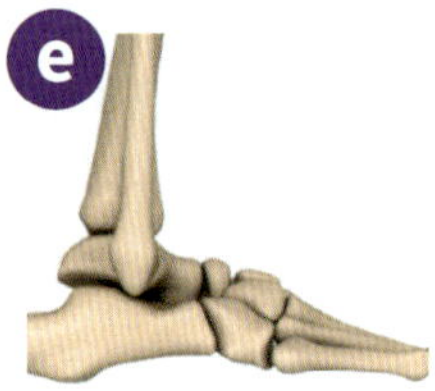

f 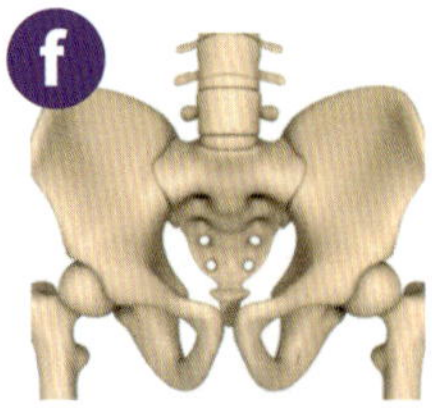

3 What activities are the joints in Activity 2 important for? Discuss with a partner.

The shoulder is important for throwing and carrying things, …

4 Look and match the sports to the protective equipment. Which parts of the body do they protect?

skiing   horse riding   skating   swimming   riding a bike

a helmet

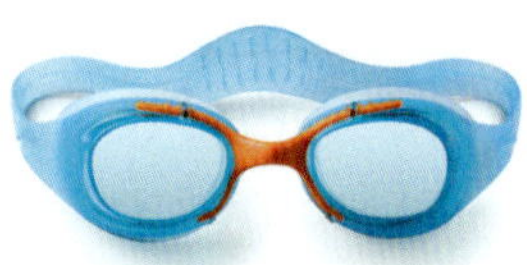
b swimming goggles

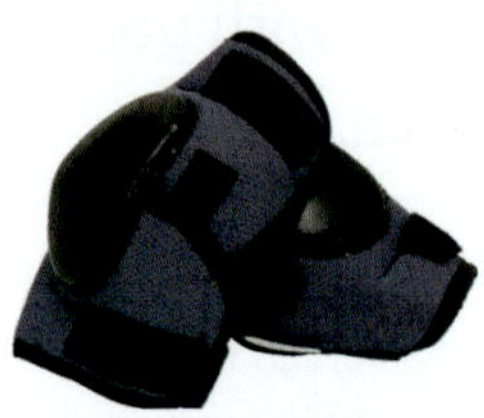
c knee and elbow pads

d boots

e goggles

5 **What activities can make our body and joints stronger? Discuss with a partner.**

6 3.12 **Listen and read. Follow the instructions with a partner.**

YOGA

Welcome to Bali, Indonesia!

On this beautiful island, yoga is very important. The people here use it to exercise and stay healthy. It's a great way to stretch your body and make your joints and muscles strong. At our centre, you can do yoga in our relaxing rooms, in the sunny garden, or on the beach! Here are a few moves we practise. Why don't you try them?

TREE POSE

Stand on one leg. Bend the other knee and put your foot on your other leg. Put your hands together above your head. Hold the position for ten seconds and breathe.

FLOWER POSE

Sit on the floor. Bend your legs. Put one foot on top of the other. Put your hands on your knees and close your eyes. Hold the position for ten seconds and breathe.

CHILD'S POSE

Kneel on the floor and sit back on your feet. Bring your head down to rest on the floor. Stretch your arms out in front of you. Hold the position for ten seconds and breathe.

7 **Read and write.**

This pose is called the warrior pose. Write instructions to explain how to do this pose. Use the words in the box. Then test your instructions on a partner.

stand	turn	raise	bend	stretch

mission STAGE 3

Add some healing tips to your health plan.

- With your partner, think about some ways to stay healthy.

Breathe slowly to keep calm.

Get lots of rest to have energy the next day.

- Add these ideas to your health plan.

My mission diary
Activity Book page 30

1 **Read these words. Which of them can you find in the pictures?**

dragon | porridge | poor | angry | girl | breakfast | roar | firewood

3.13

TOO-TOO-MOO AND THE KOMODO DRAGON

SCENE ONE

Narrator: **This is a story from Indonesia about Too-too-moo and the Komodo dragon.**

Mother: Breakfast is ready.

Too-too-moo: Oh no. Rice again!

Mother: We're poor. And remember, the dragon gets porridge. I make it for him every day. He eats all of our porridge!

Too-too-moo: I know he eats a lot, but he's the biggest dragon in the world! He's my friend.

Mother: He's a wild animal. You need to be careful!

Narrator: **And so Mother left to collect firewood to sell in the market.**

SCENE TWO

Narrator: **There was a knock on the door!**

Too-too-moo: That's the dragon. He knocks on the door louder every day.

Dragon: Too-too-moo! Where are you? I'm hungry, and I need my porridge.

Narrator: **Too-too-moo gave the dragon his breakfast. The dragon roared, and then he walked away with the porridge.**

SCENE THREE

Narrator: **The weather was hot. Nobody wanted firewood so Too-too-moo and her mother couldn't make any money. They got poorer and poorer. Soon there was no food in the little house. But still the Komodo dragon came for his porridge.**

Dragon: Too-too-moo! Where are you? I'm hungry, and I need my breakfast. Open the door! I've got a stomach-ache. I can't wait any more!

Narrator: **Too-too-moo opened the door.**

Too-too-moo: There isn't any porridge.

Narrator: **The dragon was angry. He pushed Too-too-moo. He showed his terrible teeth, and he gave a terrible roar.**

Dragon: Too-too-moo, you aren't my friend any more!

SCENE FOUR

Narrator: **At last the weather got colder. People bought firewood again. Too-too-moo's mother came home with rice and porridge.**

Mother: I'm happy that greedy dragon doesn't come here now. There is more food for us!

Too-too-moo: He wasn't greedy, Mother. He was hungry.

Mother: He's dangerous! He needs to stay in the forest where he belongs.

Narrator: **The dragon never came to the little house again. But Too-too-moo often left a bowl of porridge in the forest for his breakfast.**

2 **Why do you think Too-too-moo gives the dragon breakfast at the end?**

3 **Remember and write.**

Close your book. Work in groups. Write a simple summary of the story. Write seven sentences. Share your sentences with the class.

4 **Act out the play.**

1 Read and put the words in the table.

~~hands~~ a bus jump a horse
better older children hurt
needs long know a sport

Noun (s.)	Noun (pl.)	Adjective	Verb
	hands		

2 Choose the correct option to complete the sentences.

1 I had a headache this morning, but it ***don't*** / ***doesn't*** hurt now.

2 I look after my ***body*** / ***bodies*** by exercising every day.

3 Our shoes are ***between*** / ***in*** the cupboard.

4 My mum ***has*** / ***have*** got a backache.

5 We went to ***their*** / ***they're*** house for breakfast.

6 My friend has got longer arms ***then*** / ***than*** me.

3 Look at the picture and the title. Read and find words about the picture. Choose the right words to complete the sentences.

Legs

Before they walk, young children learn to move around __on__ their hands and knees. A horse has got four legs and a spider has got eight legs. Snakes … got any legs but they've got long bodies!

Legs can help us to jump or … , for example, when we need to catch a bus. When you play a sport like football or tennis, you sometimes hurt your knee or foot. If it's very sore, don't worry … a doctor in a hospital can make you better.

Most people have two legs, two knees, two feet and ten toes. Did you know that there are 52 bones in our feet? Are you surprised?

Example

	on	in	at
1	have	haven't	had
2	ran	running	run
3	because	and	but

Copy the word you choose on the right line.

mission in action!

Make a health advice poster.

My mission diary
Activity Book page 30

- Work in groups. Share your health plan with your group.
- Discuss the best ideas in each section.

> I think Lisa's healing tips are the best. Do you agree?

> Yes, and I think Dan's health advice is the best.

- Make a poster with some health advice for the class.

Can you remember?

1 How did Ivan hurt his toe?
2 What is Puncak Jaya?
3 Who has backache in the song?
4 What does Vicky want to do? Why can't she do it?
5 What protective equipment do you need to wear when you ride a bike?
6 Why was the Komodo dragon angry with Too-too-moo?

Review ••• Units 1–3

1 Watch the video and do the quiz.

2 (3.14) What do they need? Listen and choose.

1 a  b  c 

3 a b  c 

2 a  b  c

4 a  b  c 

3 Play the game with a partner. Choose a square. Your partner makes a sentence with that word and language from the box.

highest biggest longest strongest best clever as … as more exciting

1 me	5 mountain	9 kangaroo	13 cinema
2 a shop	6 milkshake	10 dancer	14 English
3 jump	7 river	11 lake	15 my friend
4 pop star	8 restaurant	12 books	16 elephant

Number 5 – mountain.

Mount Teide is the highest mountain in Spain.

Number 15 – my friend.

I am as clever as my friend Javier.

4 Read the text and order the pictures.

Julia and Paul's busy day

WEEK 1

31 Wednesday Mercredi Mittwock Miércoles Mercoledi

8: At eight o'clock Julia and Paul woke up. At half past eight they had cereal and pancakes for breakfast.

9: At half past nine Dad told them to 'come on!'

10: At ten o'clock Mum drove them to the countryside. They saw the hospital where Mum worked.

11: At eleven o'clock they climbed trees and they took photos. They had the best time with their mum, who taught them how to build mountains of leaves. They built five!

12: At twelve o'clock their dad made them noodles and sauce for lunch.

a

b

c

d
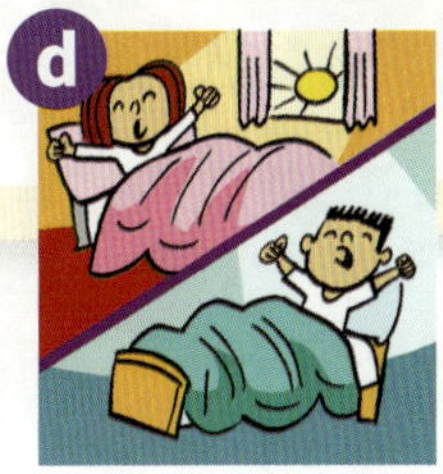

e

f

5 Cover the text and use the pictures to retell the story.

6 Copy the table and add two activities. Ask your family and complete.

Could you hop when you were three?

No, but I could dance!

	Hop	Climb trees	?	?
Me				
?				
?				

7 Write sentences. Use the information from the table in Activity 6.

My sister couldn't hop when she was three, but she could dance.

4 Fun in the jungle

1 Watch the video. Ask and answer.

What do you like to do outside?

Where's your favourite natural place?

mission Create a jungle adventure park

In this unit I will:

1. Design a map for a jungle adventure park.
2. Invent a jungle activity.
3. Add a nature area in the park.

★ Present the jungle adventure park to the class.

1 4.01 **Listen. What did May and Fred make last week?**

Diversicus is in India. This afternoon Rose is talking to Fred and May about the new show for their world tour.

2 4.02 **Say the chant.**

3 4.03 **Listen. Who says it? Say the name.**

Rose	Mrs Friendly	
May	Fred	Pablo

In India it rains a lot every day in the summer, from June to September – that's about 120 days! This time of the year is called the monsoon season.

DIVERSICUS

4.04

1 4.05 **Listen and complete. Use two words.**

1 **Look at the pictures. Which instrument do you think they play to make the sounds?**

a b c d e f

2 4.06 **How are they playing the instruments? Choose, then listen and check.**

1 A waterfall: he's playing the piano ***slowly*** / ***quickly*** and ***loudly*** / ***quietly***.
2 Bad weather at sea: he's playing the drums ***slowly*** / ***fast*** and ***loudly*** / ***quietly***.
3 Sunny island: she's playing the guitar ***loudly*** / ***quietly*** and ***slowly*** / ***quickly***.
4 Rain in the jungle: he's playing the piano ***slowly*** / ***quickly*** and ***loudly*** / ***quietly***.
5 A bird in the tree: she's singing ***beautifully*** / ***badly***.
6 Waves at night time: she's playing the piano ***loudly*** / ***quietly*** and ***slowly*** / ***quickly***.

Grammar spotlight 4.07

We mustn't talk loud**ly**. Look careful**ly** at the plants. It worked **well**.

3 **Think of your family. Read and answer.**

Who … talks quietly? eats loudly? runs fast? listens carefully?

mission STAGE 1

Design a map for a jungle adventure park.

- Work in groups. Choose a name for your park.
- Draw a map of the park.
- Label the natural features. Write a short description of each one.

This is the waterfall. The water is moving fast.

My mission diary
Activity Book page 44

1 4.08 Listen and match. Then sing the song.

Carefully, carefully, carefully, carefully
We flew to the jungle.
Carefully ...
We drove to the beach
And we sailed on the sea.
Yes, we did ...

Slowly, slowly, slowly, slowly
We fished in a river.
Slowly ...
We threw our nets
And we caught some fish.
Yes, we did ...

Quickly, quickly, quickly, quickly
We learnt to dance.
Quickly ...
We bounced and hopped.
And we skipped and kicked.
Yes, we did ...

2 **Find the past simple verbs in the song. Are they regular or irregular? Write two lists.**

3 **Play the memory game. Cover the song. Look at the pictures and say what the people did.**

1 4.10 Which is Peter's favourite animal? Listen, look and choose.

a 
b 
c 
d 
e 
f 

Grammar spotlight 4.11

Elephants can move **faster** than snakes.

Monkeys can climb **better** than tigers.

Bears can run **more quickly** than monkeys.

2 Choose two animals. Make sentences with a partner.

Animals: elephants bats tigers snakes monkeys bears

Verbs: move run jump fly swim

Adverbs: well loudly quietly quickly slowly carefully hard fast

Elephants and tigers.

Tigers can run more quickly than elephants.

mission STAGE 2

Invent a jungle activity.

- In your groups, discuss some ideas for activities to do in your jungle adventure park.

How about sailing on the lake?

Good idea, or what about fishing in the sea?

- Choose an activity and add it to your brochure.
- Write a short description and add a picture.

This activity is fishing. You sail in a boat with a guide.
You fish for two hours. You can eat the fish for dinner!

My mission diary
Activity Book page 44

From the roots to the flower

1 **Watch the video.**

2 4.12 **Listen and read. Then answer the questions.**

Plants are living things and grow almost everywhere – from the bottom of the sea to the highest mountain. What plants grow near you?

Most plants make food using sunlight. They also need water to survive, just like us!

Plants usually have three parts to them: roots, a stem and leaves. The roots take up water from the ground and the leaves take in sunlight and air around them for food. Some plants also have flowers or fruit.

1 Where do plants grow?
2 What do plants need to survive?
3 What three parts do plants usually have?
4 What other parts do plants sometimes have?
5 What's your favourite plant?

3 **Look at the diagram of the plant. Find each part in the photo.**

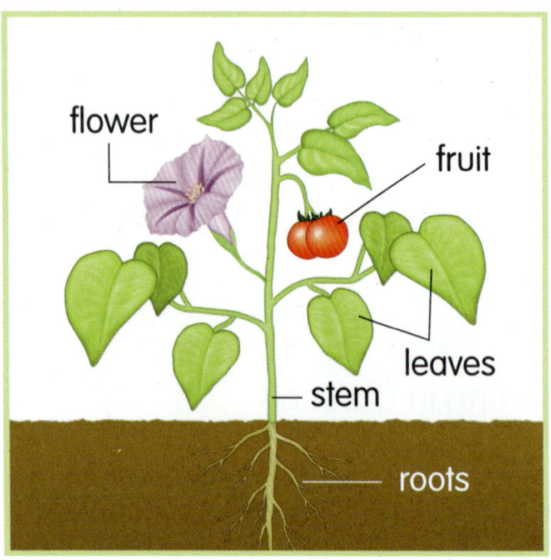

4 **Draw a plant and label it. Tell your partner about your plant.**

My favourite plant is a sunflower. This is its flower …

5 4.13 **Listen and read. Then answer the questions.**

Carnivorous plants

Like most other plants, carnivorous plants need sun, air and water to make their own food. But they also get extra nutrients by eating small animals! Here are two examples:

The Venus flytrap

Venus flytraps grow naturally in the USA but are used as house plants all over the world. They use their leaves to catch insects, like flies. The leaves close when an insect touches the tiny hairs that grow on them. The plant can then slowly eat the insect.

The Sundew plant

Sundew plants are found in the Indian rainforests. They can grow in soil that is underwater. Their leaves have sticky hairs and when an insect lands on the leaves, the sticky hairs trap them. Large sundew plants can trap and eat spiders.

Which plant ...

1 is from India?
2 is from the USA?
3 eats flies?
4 sometimes eats spiders?
5 has got sticky hairs?
6 has got tiny hairs?

6 **Create your own carnivorous plant.**

Draw and colour a carnivorous plant on a sheet of paper. Make notes about where it grows, how it catches its food and what it needs to survive. Think of a name for your plant. Then present your plant to the class.

mission STAGE 3

Add a nature area to your park.

- In your groups, discuss what plants and animals you can see in your park.

  Let's have some tigers and bears.

  OK, then we need some trees with fruit for the bears to eat.

- Add this information to your brochure.

My mission diary
Activity Book page 44

1 **Look at the pictures. What do you think the story is about? Discuss with a partner.**

4.14

THE STORY OF RAMA AND SITA

Long ago a king lived in the town of Ayodhya. He had four sons.
One day he said, 'I am getting very old now and I want my oldest son Rama to be king.'
'No!' Rama's stepmother cried. '*My* son must be king!'
The King listened to his wife, and he sadly told his oldest son to leave. Rama couldn't return to Ayodhya for 14 years.

Rama and his wife, Sita, left Ayodhya. They travelled for many days until they came to a forest. 'This looks like the perfect place to live,' said Rama. For many years, they lived happily in the forest. But there was a terrible man called Ravana in the forest. He saw Sita one day and he wanted to take her. He had a plan.

One day, Sita saw a beautiful golden deer. 'Rama, catch it for me,' she said.
When Rama left to catch the deer, Ravana came to the house dressed in a costume. He caught Sita and took her back to his palace.

When Rama returned and saw that Sita wasn't there, he searched but he couldn't find her. He decided to ask Hanuman for help. Hanuman was the great leader of the monkeys. He could fly over mountains, change size and he was very strong. 'Don't worry. I can find her quickly,' he said to Rama.

4

On her way to Ravana's palace, Sita carefully dropped her jewellery. As Hanuman flew in the sky, the pieces of jewellery were like little lights showing him the way. Soon he found Sita. She was in the garden of Ravana's palace.

Hanuman quickly told Rama where Sita was. He organised a great army of monkeys and bears. Together, they rescued her from Ravana.

Rama and Sita were happy again, and finally, after 14 years, they went back to Ayodhya. There were flowers and lanterns in the streets. The people cheered loudly and were very happy to see their real king.

In some parts of the world today, people still celebrate Rama going home.

2 Who do you think is brave/clever/unkind/helpful in the story?

3 How do you think the characters feel in these parts of the story?

- When the King tells Rama and Sita to leave Ayodhya
- When Ravana takes Sita
- When Hanuman tells Rama he found Sita
- When Rama and Sita return to Ayodhya

1 Look at the first picture and the title. Describe the picture.

2 Look at the next two pictures and tell the story.

3 Read the sentences. Match them to the correct picture in Activity 2.

1 In the evening they ate dinner outside.
2 They sang loudly after dinner.
3 Paul showed them some photos.
4 They sat in the kitchen.

4 Read the text for the first picture in Activity 1. Then choose the correct answer to complete the sentences.

Vicky and Zoe's uncle lives on a mountain next to a forest. Yesterday, the girls and their parents went there by train. When they arrived it was windy.

'Hi, Paul. It's colder here than at home!' said Vicky. 'I haven't got a scarf. I don't want a sore throat!'

'Here, take my scarf,' said Paul.

They played with the dog and then they all went quickly inside for lunch.

1 Vicky said the weather was ______________ than at her home. (*windy* / *cold* / *colder*)

2 Paul gave Vicky ______________ (*her scarf* / *his scarf* / *scarf*)

mission in action!

Present your jungle adventure park to the class.

My mission diary
Activity Book page 44

- **Show your brochure to the class.**
- **Explain your jungle activity, and why it's fun.**
- **Talk about the nature area.**
- **As a class, vote for the best jungle adventure park.**

This is our park. It's got a waterfall, a beach and a big mountain.

Our jungle activity is a fishing trip. It is an amazing experience!

Do you like tigers? Well there are lots to see in our park.

Can you remember?

1 Who is afraid of waves?
2 How should Ivan walk in the jungle?
3 Where did the children in the song go fishing?
4 What can tigers do at night time?
5 Name three parts of a plant.
6 How did Rama rescue Sita?

5 Behind the scenes

1 Watch the video. Ask and answer.

What's your favourite play or show?
Who are the characters? What do they look like?

mission **Prepare a performance**

In this unit I will:

1. Design a costume.
2. Create a set and some props.
3. Make a mask.

★ Write a scene and put on a performance.

1 5.01 **Listen. What is the name of the new show?**

2 5.02 **Say the chant.**

3 **Play the describing game.**

Be Curious about Greece

Would you like to dress up like an ancient Greek? You need to wear a chiton – that's a big square made of wool – and a belt. The Greeks didn't usually wear shoes but sometimes they wore leather sandals.

DIVERSICUS

5.03

1 5.04 **Listen to the sentences and say the answers.**

1 Read the text. What clothes does Robin describe?

These are the [1]~~clothes~~ for my costume. The trousers are [2]... of paper. They're [3]... purple with yellow [4]... . I've got yellow and purple [5]... shoes. They're made of [6]... . My helmet [7]... made of gold.

Robin

Grammar spotlight

5.05

What's it made of?	It**'s made of** gold.
What are the wings **made of**?	The wings **are made of** paper.

2 Read Activity 1 again and choose the correct answer. Use the words in the box.

~~clothes~~ striped bright made rubber is spots

3 Describe the costume in the picture.

He's wearing a black hat. It's made of …

mission STAGE 1

Design a costume.

- Choose a character from a play, film or book.
- Design a costume for the character. Think about what it's made of.
- Write a description of your costume and what it's made of.
- In groups, talk about your costume.

This is my design for a Peter Pan costume. He's wearing a hat. It's made of green paper …

My mission diary

Activity Book page 56

1 5.06 **Listen and match the materials to the numbers. Then sing the song.**

Making, making, making,
Making all day long.
Card, metal glass,
plastic, wool and wood.

Cut them up, cut them out,
Colour in, and glue!

We make, we make,
we make, we make these things.

These scissors are made of **metal**,
This scarf is made of **wool**.
My box is made of **plastic**,
And my table's made of **wood**.

Chorus

That crown is made of brown **card**,
And I've got **silver** wings.
These balls are made of **glass**,
And I've got four **gold** rings.

Chorus

2 **Read and answer. Make two more riddles.**

1 It's made of paper. You read it. What is it?
2 It's made of wood. You sit on it. What is it?
3 It's made of wool. You use it to keep your neck warm. What is it?
4 It's made of gold. You wear it on your finger. What is it?

3 **Play the game. What is it?**

I can see something – it's made of wood. What is it?

Is it the teacher's desk?

Yes, that's right!

1 5.08 **Listen. What are Kelly and Sophia designing?**

2 5.09 **Listen again. What material do they use for each thing?**

sea sun clouds

Grammar spotlight

5.10

Shall we design some props?

Let's design the sea.

We could use blue paper.

3 **Read the situations. Share ideas with a partner. Use *Shall*, *Let's* and *We could*.**

1 You're at the cinema. What film do you want to watch?

2 You're in the playground. What game can you play?

3 It's your friend's birthday. What present do you want to buy for him/her?

Shall we watch a funny film?

Let's play hide and seek!

We could buy Julia a ring.

mission STAGE 2

Create a set and some props.

- Think of your character from Mission Stage 1. Make a group with different characters.
- In your groups, think of a set. Where are the characters?
- Think of some props and decide what materials you need to make them.
- Now make your set and props.

My mission diary

Activity Book page 56

Materials and properties

1 Watch the video.

2 5.11 Listen and read. Say the opposites.

This crown is made of gold. Gold is **heavy**.

This table is made of wood. Wood is **rigid**.

This ruler is made of plastic. Plastic is **flexible**.

This house is made of bricks. Bricks are **rough**.

This newspaper is made of paper. Paper is **light**.

This slide is made of metal. Metal is **smooth**.

The opposite of heavy is …

3 Read and say.

1 Find something flexible and something rigid in the classroom.

2 Think of something heavy and something light at home.

3 Think of something rough and something smooth outside.

4 Choose and say.

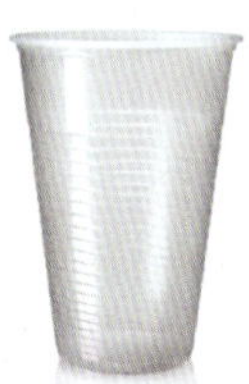

Plastic is a good material for this because it's light and rigid.

Is it a cup?

Yes it is!

5 5.12 **Listen and read. Then read the sentences and say *yes* or *no*.**

A theatre workshop

In our theatre group, we use different materials to make our costumes, props and sets. We use materials with different **properties**. Some materials are flexible and light. Some materials are rigid and strong. It's important to use materials that are safe.

We make masks with papier-mâché. It's flexible and light because it is made of paper, glue and water. You can paint the masks and decorate them with lots of different things.

Today we're making Greek masks. Theatre was very important in Ancient Greece. Most cities had a theatre and people went there to watch comedies (funny shows) or tragedies (sad or serious shows). The actors used masks to show different emotions more clearly. Some masks were double-sided, which means they could have one face on one side and a different one on the other side. Let's make happy and sad double-sided masks!

1 All materials are flexible and soft.
2 Papier-mâché is made with paper, glue and water.
3 You can't paint papier-mâché.
4 People in Ancient Greece didn't like the theatre.
5 Tragedies were usually serious shows.
6 You can have two different emotions on double-sided masks.

mission STAGE 3

Make a mask.

- In groups, read the instructions.
- Design and then make a mask for your character.
- Tell the class about your mask.

My mask is very light. It's made of papier-mâché.

My mask is bright purple with gold stripes.

Instructions

1. Cut a newspaper into strips.
2. Mix water and glue in a bowl.
3. Put the paper strips (one by one) in the bowl and cover them with the glue.
4. Put the strips on a plastic mask.
5. When it's dry, paint and decorate your mask.

My mission diary
Activity Book page 56

1 **Look at the pictures. What do you think the story is about? Discuss with a partner.**

5.13

THE MYTH OF ICARUS

One morning on the island of Crete, Icarus and his father Daedalus were in their workshop. Daedalus was an inventor. Suddenly, King Minos arrived and he spoke to Daedalus.
'I'd like you to build me a labyrinth,' he said. 'I want to put that Minotaur inside it.' The Minotaur was a terrible monster. He had the head of a bull and the body of a man.

King Minos was pleased when he saw Daedalus's work. He put the Minotaur inside the labyrinth. Then he locked Daedalus and Icarus inside a tower. 'What are you doing?' said Daedalus. 'Well,' said the King, 'you know the secret of how to get out of the labyrinth. And I don't want anyone else to know it.'

Daedalus and his son felt sad. Days passed, then Daedalus had an idea. He collected feathers from the birds that flew to the window of the tower. Then he made wings with the feathers. He used wax from a candle to stick the feathers together.

Daedalus told Icarus what to do. 'Follow me. Don't go too high because the sun will melt the wax in your wings. Don't go too low because the sea will make the feathers in your wings wet. Are you ready? Go!' Daedalus and Icarus jumped out of the window. They flew away from the island, and away from King Minos.

Daedalus flew in front, Icarus followed behind. Icarus loved flying. He was just like a bird! He forgot his father's words and he flew higher and higher. But as he got nearer to the sun, the wax between the feathers began to melt.

When Daedalus looked behind him, he couldn't see his son. 'Icarus!' he shouted. '*Icarus!* Where are you?' Daedalus looked down. There were feathers in the sea. Daedalus went to the nearest island. He sat and looked at the sea for a long time, and he felt sad for his son. That island is now called Icaria, and the sea around it is called the Icarian Sea.

2 Read and answer.

1 Do you like the story?
2 What is the most exciting part?
3 What is the saddest part?
4 Do you know any other Greek myths? Who are the characters? What happens?

3 Act out with a partner.

Imagine you are Icarus and Daedalus in the tower. Talk about how to escape.

How can we get out of here?

We could …

OK, let's try to…

1 Finish these sentences.

I like reading / listening to stories about …

My favourite kind of costume is …

I don't like costumes made of …

The best objects to make are …

I'd like to have a … made of …

2 Look at these pictures. They tell a story. Read and say *yes* or *no*.

1 A boy is putting on a robot costume with his mum. His name is Charlie.

2 Charlie is at a competition. It's four o'clock.

3 Charlie is buying his favourite toy monster. His mum is reading a comic.

4 Charlie is standing next to two people in costumes. He's crying.

5 Charlie is the winner! He's got some DVDs and he's happy. A man is taking a photo.

Talk about all the pictures.

3 5.14 Listen. Now you finish the story.

mission in action!

Write a scene and put on a performance.

- Plan and write a scene in your groups
- What's the name of the show?
- Who are the characters?
- What are they doing?
- What do they say?
- Where are they?

My mission diary

Activity Book page 56

- Talk about your costumes, props and masks.

My crown is made of gold paper and my mask is made of card.

- Act out your scene for the class.

Can you remember?

1 Which circus artist is wearing a spotted shirt?
2 What are the practice wings made of?
3 Say something made of plastic.
4 What do Kelly and Sophia use to make the clouds?
5 Name three materials that are flexible.
6 Why did Icarus fall into the sea?

6 Classroom stars

1 Watch the video. Ask and answer.

What are your favourite subjects at school?

Why do you like these subjects?

mission **Have a school prize-giving ceremony**

In this unit I will:

1. Describe how to be good at a subject.
2. Find out what my classmates are good at.
3. Make a prize for each subject or activity.

★ Give prizes to my classmates.

1 6.01 Listen. What homework does Miguel give the children?

2 6.02 Say the chant.

3 Write your school timetable. Ask and answer.

What have we got at nine o'clock on Tuesdays?

We've got maths.

What time is the break?

It's at half past ten.

Be Curious about Turkey

Turkish is the first language of more than 70 million people. Some words in English come from Turkish: kayak, kiosk, yoghurt. Do you know any words in English from your language?

DIVERSICUS

6.03

1 6.04 **Listen. Who says it?**

1 **Look at the picture. Are the children interested in this subject?**

2 **Read. Complete the text with *should* or *shouldn't*.**

To do well at school you [1]should arrive at your classroom at the right time. You [2]... have your books, notebook and pencil and you [3]... always listen carefully to your teacher. You [4]... eat in class and you [5]... talk to your classmates when the teacher's giving the lesson. You [6]... put your feet on the desks or the chairs, and you [7]... pass notes during class time. You [8]... do your homework and projects as well as you can and you [9]... study hard. You [10]... copy in exams. You [11]... have fun during your break.

Grammar spotlight

6.05

You **should** listen to your teacher.

You **shouldn't** talk when your teacher's giving the lesson.

Should you copy in exams? No, you **shouldn't**

3 **Read and write four sentences.**

Paul goes to bed late. It's difficult for him to study at school. What should he do? What shouldn't he do?

mission STAGE 1

Describe how to be good at a subject.

- Choose a subject. Write three things you should do and three things you shouldn't do to learn this subject well.
- Find other people in the class who chose the same subject and make a group.
- Compare your lists and create one list with the five best ideas.

In geography, you should read maps.

You shouldn't copy information from the Internet.

My mission diary

Activity Book page 68

1 6.06 Listen and match. Then sing the song.

I've got a **laptop**,
With some great **apps**.
It's got an **e-book** and wifi
And a special **rucksack**.

There's an online **dictionary**
To see what words mean.
There's no **bin** in my room,
It's there on the screen.

I can do it all …
On my brilliant laptop.

I do my homework.
I use the **Internet**.
I find safe **websites**
On the World Wide Web.

I can copy and cut,
Paste a photo or two.
I don't need **scissors**
And I don't need **glue**.
Chorus

2 6.08 Listen. Write the words.

3 Play the game. Ask and answer. Then tell the class.

Find someone who …

1. reads e-books
2. has got a laptop
3. has got a rucksack
4. plays computer games
5. uses a dictionary
6. doesn't use the Internet to do homework

Do you read e-books?

No, I don't.

Peter doesn't read e-books.

Let's talk about homework. What do you use to do your homework?

1 **Look at the picture. What do you think the boy is good at?**

2 6.09 **Listen and answer the questions.**

1 What's David's favourite subject?
2 What's he good at?
3 What isn't he good at?

Grammar spotlight 6.10

I'**m good at** maths.
Are you **good at** sport?
I'**m** not very **good at** drawing.

3 **What are your friends good at? Ask and answer with five friends.**

Christina, what are you good at?
I'm good at taking photos.
Are you good at music?
No, I'm not very good at music.

4 **Write about what your friends are good at.**

Christina's good at taking photos.

mission STAGE 2

Find out what your classmates are good at.

- In your groups, share your notes from Activities 3 and 4.
- Ask and answer to find out what every person in the class is good at.

What is Sara good at?
She's good at football.

My mission diary
Activity Book page 68

Where are we?

1 Watch the video.

2 6.11 **Listen and read. Then look at the maps and match.**

political map physical map street map

In geography, we learn about maps. We need maps to find places and show distances between places.

There are different types of maps, including:

- **political maps**, which show borders between countries or between areas inside a country;
- **street maps**, which show the different roads in an area;
- **physical maps**, which show natural features in an area, like rivers, mountains and lakes.

1

2

3

3 6.12 **Listen and read the information about maps. Answer the questions.**

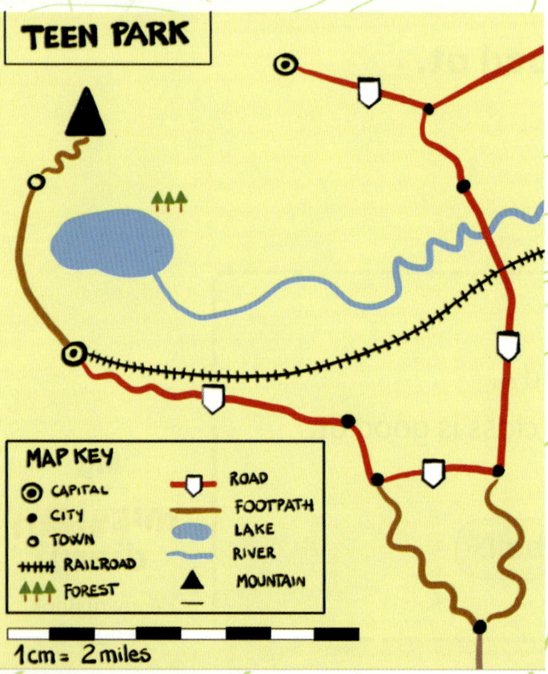

Maps

All maps have a **title** which tells us the name of the place on the map.

The **scale** shows the real distance between two places.

The pictures on a map are called **symbols**. They represent real things, like mountains or buildings.

The **key** explains what each symbol or colour means.

1. Find these things on the map: a river, a mountain, a lake and a forest.
2. What is the scale of the map?
3. How far is it from the forest to the lake? Use a ruler to find out.

4 6.13 Listen and read. Where is Cappadocia?

Cappadocia, Turkey, is different from any other place on Earth. It is a very high area: over 1,000 metres above the sea. There are many mountains across this area which are thousands of years old and made from volcanic rock. Some of these mountains are really high, like Kayseri, which is the highest at 3,916 metres!

Because Cappadocia is so high, the weather can change a lot. It can be very hot some days and very cold other days.

The people who lived in Cappadocia many years ago made small houses inside the mountains and rocks. You should visit it because you can explore inside the exciting houses and see how the people lived!

5 Read the text again and complete the fact file.

FACT FILE: Cappadocia	
Where is it? …	Why should you visit? …
How high is it above the sea? …	What's the highest mountain? …
What's the weather like? …	Where did the people live? …

6 Discuss with a partner. What famous natural features are there in your country?

The Pyrenees are a mountain range in Spain.

mission STAGE 3

Make a prize for each subject or activity.

- In your groups, think of a prize for each subject or activity in your Stage 2 notes.
- Design your prizes.

My mission diary

Activity Book page 68

1 **Look at the pictures. What do you think the legend in this story is about? Make predictions.**

2 **Now read and listen to the story and check your predictions.**

6.14 THE PROJECT

Katy, Mike and Harold were in the library talking about a project about Turkey. Mr Carlton, their teacher, said they could choose any topic for their project, but it should be about Turkey.

'Betty's group is doing their project about the geography of Turkey,' said Katy.

Harold was reading about Turkey on a website. 'The history of Turkey is very interesting. It was part of the Ottoman Empire!'

'Freddy's group's doing their project about that,' said Katy. 'What about science?'

'No,' said Harold. He didn't like science.

Katy looked at her timetable. 'The project's for Friday,' she said. 'Let's hurry up!' Katy had an idea. 'Our project can be about Turkish literature. I'm sure that Turkey has lots of stories and myths. These can teach us a lot about a place.'

'Great idea! We should find one on the Internet. Mr Carlton likes us to use IT,' said Mike.

'Why don't we do something original, like re-write the story as a poem? I'm good at writing poems,' said Katy. 'Mike's good at art. He can draw the pictures. And you're good at acting, Harold. You can read it to the class!'

'Perfect,' said Mike. So that's what they did!

THE MOUSE AND THE CAMEL

A mouse came out of his hole in the ground,
Into the sunlight, and looked around.
He saw that a camel was walking by,
With rope around it. The mouse didn't know why.
So he took the rope, and feeling happy,
He pulled the camel along, singing loudly!

But soon they came to a river wide,
And the mouse felt sick and strange inside.
'Oh please, Mr Camel, please help me,
I don't like water, as you can see!'
So the camel told the mouse to jump
Onto his back, and sit on his hump.

But when they got to the other side,
He said 'Get off! That's the end of your ride!
And understand, you silly little thing,
That in the desert the camel is king!'

Their project was a great success. Everyone loved it!

3 **Work in groups. Use the words in the box to help you retell the story.**

project teacher geography history idea mouse
camel rope desert river back king success

4 **The project was a success because Katy, Mike and Harold worked together in a team. When do you work in teams? Do you like working in a team?**

1 Look at the picture. Ask and answer.

1 Where are the children?
2 Count the boys.
3 Which names are boys' names?
4 Where is the teacher?
5 Count the girls.
6 Which names are girls' names?

George **Richard** **Megan**

Sophia **David** **Robert** **Katy**

2 Point to a person in the picture and ask your partner to describe him/her.

3 6.15 Listen and find the person. Say his/her name.

Richard

There are five questions but six names, so one name is extra.

mission in action!

Give prizes to your classmates.

My mission diary
Activity Book page 68

- In your groups, give your prizes to your classmates in the other groups.
- Tell them why you're giving them the prize.
- Tell them what the prize is.
- Remember to say thank you when you get your prize!

You are good at English.

Your prize is a book.

Can you remember?

1 Which was Pablo's favourite day? Why?
2 Where did Jim, Jenny and their friends go after the market?
3 Say three things you should do to do well in school.
4 What's David good at?
5 Say three types of maps.
6 Who's good at writing poems: Katy, Mike or Harold?

Review ••• Units 4–6

1 **Watch the video and do the quiz.**

2 6.16 **Listen and choose.**

1 My cousin eats very ***quickly*** / ***slowly***. She should eat more ***quickly*** / ***slowly*** as she always gets a stomach-ache!

2 My brother ***isn't*** / ***is*** good at skating. He does it very ***badly*** / ***well***! He should practise more.

3 My sister isn't good at fishing. She should do it more ***quietly*** / ***loudly*** as she's too ***loud*** / ***quiet***!

4 I'm learning to sail so I do it very ***carefully*** / ***loudly***.

5 I can kick a ball very ***hard*** / ***fast***.

3 **Talk to your partner about one of the words below, but don't say the word. Can your partner guess it?**

art

maths

history

geography

scissors

e-book

dictionary

bin

website

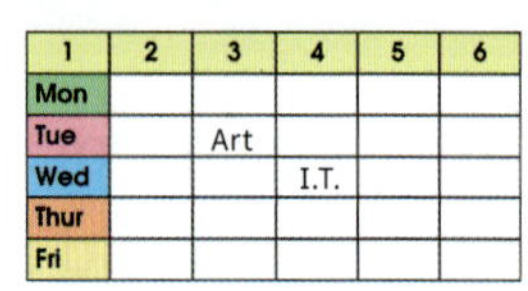

subject

You work with numbers.

Maths!

4 **Read the text. Then write *yes* or *no*. Correct the sentences that are wrong.**

We went to the theatre last night to watch the play *The Jungle Book*. The stage was so beautiful. There was a big jungle with a dark blue sky. There was a gold star and a bright moon in the sky. They were made of paper. On one side there was a light-blue waterfall made of soft material. On the other side there were four plants, two gold and two green. They were made of rubber. There were two small birds on the plants. One of the birds had spotted wings. They were made of wool! It was very clever.

1. There was an island on the stage.
   No. There was a jungle on the stage.
2. There was a dark blue sky.
3. There were two silver stars in the sky.
4. There was a bright moon.
5. There was a waterfall.
6. There were three gold plants.
7. The two birds had spotted wings.

5 **Read the text again and draw the set.**

6 **Find these objects in your house. Copy and complete the table. Write.**

	How many are there?	What are they made of?

I have nine chairs in my house. Three are made of plastic, six are made of wood.

7 When I grow up ...

1 **Watch the video. Ask and answer.**

What jobs do people in your family do?
Would you like to do these jobs? Why/why not?

mission Choose your dream job

In this unit I will:

1. Compare different jobs.
2. Add personality descriptions to each job.
3. Discuss the everyday tasks of a job.

★ Go to a job fair.

1 7.01 Listen. Why are these people talking to the children?

2 7.02 Say the chant.

3 7.03 Listen again and complete.

photographer artists driver singer designers cook journalist acrobat

1 Betty Parks is a … .
2 Oliver's a … .
3 Su-Lin's mum's a … .
4 Su-Lin's grandparents are … and … .
5 Jenny's dad's a … .
6 Pablo's uncle's an … and a … .

Be Curious about Spain

The oldest restaurant in the world is in Madrid. It's called Casa Botín and it opened in 1725. The famous artist Francisco de Goya was a waiter there!

DIVERSICUS

7.04

1 7.05 **Listen and say *yes* or *no*.**

1 Look at the picture. What's the boy doing?

2 Read and answer.

William's good at art and he loves taking photos. He wants to be a photographer when he grows up. Last year he joined a club for young photographers. Every year they have a competition for the best photo, and if you win, you get a big prize. If William wins, he wants to buy a fantastic new camera so he can take much better photos. If he doesn't win the competition, he hopes to get a new camera for his birthday.

1 What does William want to be when he grows up?
He wants to be a photographer when he grows up.
2 What do you get if you win the competition?
3 What does William want to buy if he wins?
4 What does he hope to get if he doesn't win the competition?

Grammar spotlight

7.06

When you **dance**, you **look** in the mirror.

If you **win**, you **get** a big prize.

If William **wins**, he **wants** to buy a fantastic new camera.

3 Answer the questions. What do you do if …

1 you've got a cold?
2 you haven't got a pen?
3 your homework is difficult?
4 the waiter brings you the wrong food?

mission STAGE 1

Compare different jobs.

- Work with a partner. Choose three jobs you know.
- Individually, write a short description of each job. What do they do? Where do they work?
- Compare your descriptions with your partner.

Waiters work in restaurants and cafés. When the customers finish their food, the waiter takes the plates.

My mission diary
Activity Book page 82

1 7.07 **Listen and point. Say the names. Then sing the song.**

I know a man.
Oh, yeah. What's he like? ...
He's **interesting** and **kind**,
Interesting and **kind**.

I know a boy.
Oh, yeah. What's he like? ...
He's **friendly** and **clever**,
Friendly and **clever**.

I know a dog.
Oh, yeah. What's it like? ...
It's **lazy** and **lovely**,
Lazy and **lovely**.

I know a girl.
Oh, yeah. What's she like? ...
She's **unkind** and **unfriendly**,
Unkind and **unfriendly**.

I know a woman.
Oh, yeah. What's she like? ...
She's **popular** and **brave**,
Popular and **brave**.

2 7.09 **Listen and say the word.**

3 **Close the book. Ask and answer about the people in the song.**

What's Sophie like?

She's brave.

Who's lazy?

Rex is lazy.

1 7.10 **Listen. Why is Frank's family in the newspaper?**

Grammar spotlight 7.11

What does your grandad **look like**?	He's very tall and he's got short, grey hair.
What**'s** your uncle **like**?	He's very friendly.

2 Ask and answer about Frank's family.

What does Frank's uncle look like?

He's got short dark hair and a beard.

3 Ask your friends about their families.

cousin uncle aunt grandfather grandmother sister brother mum dad

What does your dad look like?

He's got long brown hair and blue eyes.

What's your brother like?

He's lazy and kind.

mission STAGE 2

Add personality descriptions to each job.

- With your partner, discuss what personality each job needs.

What are teachers like?

I think teachers are friendly and clever.

- Write a personality description for each job.

My mission diary

Activity Book page 82

Time detectives

1 **Watch the video. Then read the text.**

Do you like investigating the past? You might like to be an archaeologist then! Archaeologists look for things that could give us information about how people lived in the past.

2 **Talk to a partner about the pictures. Which pictures interest you? Why?**

3 **Look at the pictures. What is the girl looking at in the museum? How old do you think the objects are?**

4 **What do these objects tell us about this time in history?**

5 7.12 **Listen and read Paula's story and answer the questions.**

Beautiful paintings

Bison, Altamira Caves, Santander, Spain

My dad is an archaeologist. Last year, he visited Spain. There is lots of work for an archaeologist in Spain because it's got many examples of how people lived in the past. Its history is very old! My dad went to the Altamira Caves. The caves are famous because archaeologists discovered the first cave paintings there in 1895. My dad says that in the past, people told stories using art. They didn't write like we do.

The paintings are over 14,000 years old. Many of the paintings on the cave walls show animals and people hunting. In one cave, a really big painting showed a bison (a type of animal). We think the paintings tell the story of how people hunted.

There were no paints or paintbrushes then so the cave people used the things they found around them. They used sticks, leaves and animal hair for their brushes. They made paint with fruits, plants and blood!

When I grow up I want to be an archaeologist like my father. He has a very interesting job and he sees amazing things!

Paula White

1 What job does Paula's father do?
2 Where did he go to visit the caves?
3 Why did they paint on the walls of the caves?
4 What did the early cave people paint pictures of?
5 How did they make their paint?

6 **Make your own 'cave painting' to show how life is today.**

mission STAGE 3

Discuss the everyday tasks of a job.

- With your partner, choose one of your jobs.
- Individually, make a list of all the tasks someone with that job does.
- Compare your list with your partner.

My mission diary
Activity Book page 82

1 Work in small groups. Talk about when people are brave. Do you know anyone who is brave?

2 Look at the pictures. Who do you think is brave? Read and check.

7.13 DON QUIXOTE, SANCHO AND THE WINDMILLS

Narrator: A long time ago in Spain in a land called La Mancha, there was a quiet village with a large house. The man who lived in the house was called Alonso Quijano. Alonso read books all day about brave knights. He read so much that sometimes he forgot to eat or sleep. He dreamed about saving women in danger and fighting dragons. One day he decided to become a knight and he changed his name to Don Quixote. He put on his grandfather's armour and he rode his horse Rocinante. He asked his good friend Sancho Panza to join him and he promised to pay him lots of money in return.
This story is about one of their fantastic adventures …

Quixote: Look, Sancho! Our next great adventure. Can you see them?

Sancho: What?

Quixote: Thirty or forty giants over there.

Sancho: What giants?

Quixote: Over there! Look how long their arms are. They're moving in all directions.

Sancho: Dear friend. You think they look like giants but they're windmills and the arms you can see are their sails blowing in the wind.

Quixote: Be quiet, Sancho! And prepare my horse for me! If you are afraid, you can stay here.
Sancho: No, I'm not afraid. What I mean is …
Quixote: Let's go, Rocinante.

[Don Quixote and his horse ride quickly towards the windmills.]

Quixote: Don't run, unkind giants!

[The windmill catches Don Quixote and Rocinante and then throws them down.]

Sancho: Friend! Are you alright? I told you that …
Quixote: Be quiet, Sancho! Someone changed the giants into windmills. It's magic!
Sancho: Yes, yes, my friend. Let me help you.

Narrator: And they continued on their journey to find their next adventure.

3 Work in groups of three. Act out the story.

1 Put the words in the right group.

head beans ~~actor~~ strawberry photographer badminton skating moustache soup finger farmer journalist sailing waiter

food	jobs	sports	body

	actor		

2 Look at the example. Which words help you to choose the answer?

This person uses a camera at work. a photographer

3 Write the words that help you in these sentences.

1 You have to remember a lot of words for this job and you work on a stage. an actor

2 This is a popular job for people who can paint or draw very well. an artist

3 This is a good job if you like food and you want to work in the kitchen at a restaurant. a cook

4 There are lots of these at a concert for a singer and they are different colours. lights

5 A person with this job uses a car and can work in a city or for a famous pop star! a driver

4 Play the game.

Places: circus school zoo museum station

The home: hall balcony garden bathroom desk

This is where acrobats work.

The circus.

Copy the words carefully and spell them correctly too!

mission in action!

Go to a job fair.

- Move around the classroom.
- In pairs, ask and answer about your classmates' jobs.

What does an actor do?

- Say what you think about the job.

I wouldn't like to be an actor. I'm not good at performing on stage.

- Choose your favourite job.

My mission diary
Activity Book page 82

Can you remember?

1 Which Diversicus character's grandfather is an artist?
2 How did Miguel buy the tickets for the boat ride?
3 Why did William enter the photography competition?
4 What's the name of the lovely and lazy dog?
5 What does an archaeologist do?
6 What did Don Quixote think the windmills were?

8 City break

1 Watch the video. Ask and answer.

What do you like to do in the city?
Where's your favourite place in the city?

mission Create a guide to a town

In this unit I will:

1. Make a map of a town.
2. Ask and give directions.
3. Add some green spaces to the town.
4. Give a presentation about the town.

1 8.01 **Listen. Who helps the Friendly family?**

2 8.02 **Say the chant.**

3 8.03 **Listen and complete.**

left river lorry right ~~park~~ east south

1. The Friendly family need to get to the lorry park .
2. The lorry park is next to the …
3. They are in the north, but they need to go …
4. When they get to Road 95, they turn …
5. On Road 95 they need to go …
6. When they get to Road 9, they turn …
7. Ivan is in Rose's …

Be Curious about the USA

The tallest rollercoaster in the world is near New York City. It's called Kingda Ka and it's really fast and goes very high. It goes up to 139m – that's as tall as 42 elephants!

DIVERSICUS

8.04

1 8.05 **Listen and say *yes* or *no*.**

Grammar spotlight

8.06

I'**m going to take** my umbrella.

It **isn't going to rain**.

What **are** we **going to see** first?

1 Look at the picture. What are the children learning to do?

2 Read and complete the text with these words.

isn't ~~next~~ We're On it's stay going to

Hi George

Sorry you couldn't come to school today. I hope you're better now. Mr Brown asked me to tell you about the plans for the school trip [1] next week. [2] ... going to go camping next Friday, and we're going to [3] ... in the forest for two days. [4] ... Saturday morning we're going to take a boat ride on the lake, and afterwards we're [5] ... have lunch in the park next to the waterfall. In the afternoon some of us are going to have a sailing lesson and the others are going to have a windsurfing lesson. You have to choose before you go. There [6] ... going to be time for a swim. Mr Brown says [7] ... going to be sunny, but the water's very cold.

See you soon. Love, Katy

3 Imagine you're George or Katy. Which water sport are you going to choose? Why? Write an email to Mr Brown.

mission STAGE 1

Make a map of a town.

- Work in small groups. Decide which places you're going to have in your town. Decide which materials you're going to use to make the map.

We're going to use cardboard for the sports centre.

- Make the buildings and label them, then label directions on the map.

My mission diary

Activity Book page 94

1 8.07 Listen and match. Then sing the song.

We're at the **airport**,
New York, JFK.
We're going to see the **buildings**,
New York, New York.

We're going to go to the **bank**,
To get some **money**.
Then to the **post office**,
To buy some **stamps**.
New York, New York.

We need a new toothbrush,
And some new toothpaste.
We need to find a **chemist's**.
New York, New York.

Let's go to a **theatre**,
Visit a **museum**,
Near the **university**,
And see some art.
New York, New York.

There's a brilliant **hotel**,
With a **restaurant**.
We're going to have a burger.
New York, New York.

c

d

e

f

g

h

i

j

k

l

2 Imagine you're going to go to New York. What are you going to see? What are you going to do? Tell your partner.

3 Write an email to your friend about your plans in Activity 2.

Let's talk about cities. What do you think is the best thing about the city?

1 8.09 **Listen and follow the directions on the map.**

Grammar spotlight 8.10

We should go **into** the park **through** North Gate.

across, **into**, **out of**, **over**, **past**, **round**, **through**

across

over

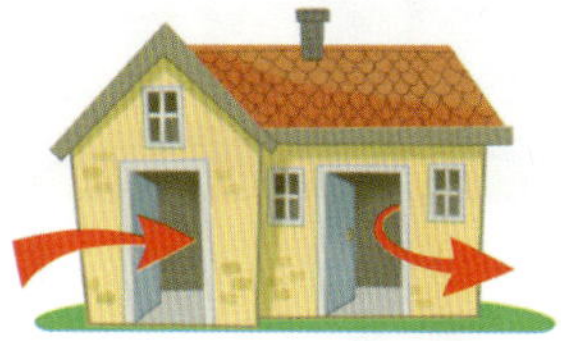
into out of

through

round

past

2 **Look at the map. Give your partner directions from Black Bridge to the theatre.**

3 **Write directions from your house to the school.**

mission STAGE 2

Ask and give directions.

- Work with a partner.
- Use your map. Ask and give directions in your town.

I am at the post office. How do I get to the hotel?

Go across the bridge and past the museum. The hotel is on the right.

My mission diary

Activity Book page 94

Home, sweet home

1 Watch the video.

2 8.11 Listen and read. Then look at the pictures. Which show villages, towns or cities?

a 

b 

c 

Almost every country in the world has cities, towns and villages. In **cities**, the population is usually over 300,000 people. They have many buildings and roads.

Towns usually have over 1,000 people. They are smaller than cities and their roads are not as wide as city roads.

Villages usually have 1,000 people or fewer. They have a few small buildings and roads, and often have more natural areas such as rivers.

d 

e 

f 

3 Do you live in a city, a town or a village? Where would you like to live? Why? Tell a partner.

4 Talk about the good and bad things about living in a village and living in a city. Use the photos to help you.

5 8.12 **Listen and read the fact file. Talk about how it is different from where you live.**

Fact file: New York City

Location	North-east coast of the USA. On the Atlantic Ocean.
Size	789 square kilometres.
Population	Around 8.5 million people.
Climate	Very hot in some parts of the year and very cold in others.
City characteristics	City of skyscrapers – over 6,000 high-rise buildings. Very busy city. People from all over the world live here.
Places of interest	Manhattan The Statue of Liberty Brooklyn Bridge The Empire State Building Times Square The Museum of Modern Art Central Park

6 **Write a fact file about a city, town or village in your own country. Use the headings in Activity 5 to help you.**

mission STAGE 3

Add some green spaces to your town.

- In groups, choose some green spaces to include in your town.
- Use symbols to add them to your map and create a key.

My mission diary
Activity Book page 94

1 **Look at the pictures and answer the questions.**

1. Where do you think the family are?
2. What do you think they're doing?
3. Are you good at giving directions?

8.13

THE ROAD TO HOPE

I'm Kay and he's Jay, and we're both here today,
To talk about our life in the USA.
Our country is big and our country is wide,
Over two thousand miles from side to side.

Last year we went on a trip in the car.
'Don't worry,' said Mum, 'we aren't going to go far.'
We wanted to visit this small town called Hope,
Where Grandma was born, she's called Sue-Ella Cope.

But the road was so long and it went on and on,
Over bridge after bridge until Dad said, 'We're wrong.
This isn't the way to Hope town, do you know,
We shouldn't be going this way, no, no, no.'

Dad shouted, 'We should go west.'
But Mum said, 'No, east is best.'
We sat in silence, and looked at Yvonne,
Who picked up the laptop and turned it on.

Our sister so small, so clever, so kind,
Searched her laptop and tried hard to find,
An app that would help us all get to the town.
'Go left,' she said now, 'and go up please, not down.'

We went left at the shops and straight on at the light.
The day was so warm and the sun was so bright.
'Look!' said Yvonne. 'Can you all see the sign?
I'm quite good at finding directions online.'

We laughed and we laughed and said, 'Well done, Yvonne,
We're here in the town, and we didn't go wrong.
From now on it's your job to show us the way.
Thank you for helping us get here today.'

2 Choose the word to describe the family's emotions. Why do they feel this way?

1 The family are going on a trip. Everyone is ***bored*** / ***excited*** / ***tired***.
2 Mum and Dad don't know how to get to Hope. They're ***happy*** / ***angry*** / ***surprised***.
3 Jay and Kay don't know how to get to Hope. They're ***afraid*** / ***bored*** / ***happy***.
4 Yvonne knows how to get to Hope. She's ***calm*** / ***worried*** / ***tired***.

1 **Look at the pictures in Activity 2. Find and point to six things that are different.**

In my picture, the waiter is putting a milkshake on the table but in your picture, the waiter is putting some cake on the table.

2 8.14 **Listen. Does the girl talk about the same differences as you?**

Listen carefully and talk about six differences. Try to use full sentences.

mission in action!

Give a presentation about your town.

My mission diary
Activity Book page 94

- Describe the buildings and their location in the town using the map.
- Explain how to get to different places in the town.
- Describe all the green spaces in the town.
- As a class, vote to choose the best town.

Can you remember?

1 Where did the Friendly family need to get to?
2 Where were Rose and the children when it started to rain?
3 Where can you buy some stamps?
4 Name three buildings you don't usually see in a village.
5 What's the population of New York City?
6 What did Yvonne use to find directions?

9 Let's travel!

1 **Watch the video. Ask and answer.**

Where did you go for your last holiday?
What did you do there?

mission Organise a summer camp

In this unit I will:

1. Prepare a three-day timetable.
2. Describe the activities at the summer camp.
3. Pack a bag for the summer camp.

★ Write a review about the summer camp.

1 9.01 **Listen. What's the hero called?**

2 9.02 **Say the chant.**

3 9.03 **Listen and say *yes* or *no*.**

Be Curious about Mexico

The smallest dogs in the world get their name from a big state in Mexico: Chihuahua. Chihuahua dogs are very little, but they can be very noisy when they are excited!

DIVERSICUS

9.04

1 9.05 **Listen. Who says it?**

Grammar spotlight

9.06

Rose got really wet **before** I gave her my umbrella.

He ran really fast **when** Fred came out of the trees.

After we met Grandma's sister in China, we ate the fantastic noodles.

1 Look at the photos. What are the children doing?

2 Choose the words to complete the text.

Well, this is our last article for the school newspaper. Before we [1]*go* / *arrive* on holiday, we should remember some of the most exciting things from the last year.

Our first trip was to the funfair. After we [2]*get off* / *got off* one of the rides, we [3]*buy* / *bought* this amazing photo.

One of our favourite trips was when we [4]*visited* / *visit* the fire station. [5]*After* / *If* we [6]*meet* / *met* the brave firefighters there, we put on their helmets. George [7]*took* / *take* this photo.

Last month we [8]*go* / *went* camping in the forest. We took a boat ride on the lake [9]*when* / *before* we had a windsurfing lesson. It [10]*was* / *is* brilliant.

See you next year!

George and Katy

3 Ask and answer. What did you do ...

1. when you got home from school yesterday?
2. after you got up this morning?
3. when you arrived at school this morning?
4. before you had dinner last night?

mission STAGE 1

Prepare a three-day timetable.

- In groups, discuss some ideas for activities for your summer camp.

On day one, let's go hiking after breakfast.

Great idea! And for lunch let's go to the place where they make the best pancakes.

- Write your three-day timetable.

My mission diary
Activity Book page 106

1 9.07 **Listen and find the words from the song in the picture. Then sing the song.**

This year's tour is over.
Yes, it is, we're on our way …
We're packing all our boxes
And the tent, the enormous tent.

I need to find my **pyjamas**
Before I pack my **trainers**.
I need to pack my **suitcase**,
Yes, I do. Yes, I do.

Chorus

After I pack my **rucksack**,
We're going to go on holiday.
We're going to go to the beach,
To make **sandcastles** by the sea.

Chorus

Don't forget to send these **postcards**,
With **views** of Mexico.
Remember to put the **stamp** on,
And take it to the post office.

Chorus

2 9.09 **Listen and write.**

3 **Imagine you're going to go on holiday next week. Ask and answer.**

What are you going to pack in your suitcase?

I'm going to pack my trainers.

Why?

Because I'm going to play football.

1 9.10 **Listen. What's Sophia going to do on holiday? Say three things.**

Grammar spotlight

9.11

You're going to be **tired** at the end of your holiday.

Yes, it is going to be **tiring**.

2 What do you think about these things? Ask and answer.

going to a museum | going to the beach | exams | jungles | camping | studying | shopping | computer games | football | dancing

boring | interesting | frightening | tiring | exciting | surprising

What do you think about going to a museum?

I think it's interesting.

3 Tell your partner about the last time you were …

1 bored
2 frightened
3 tired
4 excited
5 surprised
6 interested

The last time I was excited was when I went to a funfair.

mission STAGE 2

Describe the activities at the summer camp.

- In your groups, discuss the activities in your timetable.

There's a walk on the beach and a sandcastle competition after the walk.

That's going to be exciting!

- Write a short description for each activity.

My mission diary

Activity Book page 106

Cross-curricular

North, south, east and west

1 Watch the video.

2 Look at the pictures. What activities are the children doing?

1

2

3

4

5

6

3 Which activities do you think are exciting, frightening or tiring? What do you like doing in the countryside?

4 What should you take with you when you go hiking? Why? Choose and tell a partner.

When you go hiking, you should take a map so you don't get lost.

5 Look at the pictures. How can the sky help you find your way if you haven't got a compass?

6 9.12 Listen and read Jasmin's diary. What did they use to find their way?

Saturday July 15th

Day five in Mexico! Today was very interesting. We went to visit a pyramid at the top of the Tepozteco Mountain in Morelos. It was a beautiful walk. We went past waterfalls and amazing rainforests! We walked very far because the pyramid is very high up the mountain. On the way, we saw lots of lizards. We rested at the top of the mountain and we had a picnic. The view was lovely; we could look down on the beautiful town of Tepoztlan. Danny took lots of pictures.

When we were preparing to go back down the mountain, disaster happened! Danny fell and our compass broke. Oh no! How could we find our way with no compass?

We couldn't look at the stars because it was day time. Danny wanted to make a compass but we didn't have the right materials. Then Mum found the solution. The sun was getting lower in the sky. Of course! The sun rises in the east and it sets in the west. Now we knew where west was and it was easy to find south.

We arrived back at the hotel hot and dirty, but safe. Mum is now the superhero of the family. What's going to happen to us tomorrow?

7 Read the diary again and answer the questions.

1 Which country is Jasmin visiting?
2 What's the name of the mountain which they climbed?
3 What was at the top of the mountain?
4 What happened to the compass?
5 Why didn't they use the stars to find their way?
6 Why didn't they make a compass?

mission STAGE 3

Pack a bag for the summer camp.

- In your groups, discuss what items you're going to need for each activity.

For hiking, we're going to need a compass and some boots.

For visiting the town hall, we're going to need a camera and some money.

- Write a final list of things to pack for the summer camp.

My mission diary
Activity Book page 106

1 **What do these words mean? Discuss with a partner. Use the pictures or a dictionary to help you.**

volcano shape tent warrior tribe broken heart

2 **What's the story about? Make predictions. Then read and check.**

9.13

THE STORY OF POPOCATEPETL AND IZTACCIHUATL

Harry and Sophie were on holiday in Mexico with their cousins, Jaime and Alicia. Before they went home, they wanted to climb Popocatepetl. Popocatepetl is a volcano not very far from Mexico City. The night before the climb, they camped at the bottom of the volcano with their mountain climbing guide. Harry and Jaime looked up at the volcano covered with snow.

'It's going to be exciting tomorrow,' said Jaime. Harry was excited, too.

'What a strange shape that other mountain is,' said Sophie suddenly. 'It looks like a woman lying down.'

The guide looked where she was pointing. 'Yes,' he said. 'It does. That's a volcano, too. Let's put up the tents before it gets dark, and then I can tell you the story of the two volcanoes.'

After they put up the tents, they all sat down and they listened to the story of Popocatepetl and Iztaccihuatl. It was very interesting.

Text type: A narration and legend

'Long ago, there was a beautiful princess called Iztaccihuatl. Popocatepetl was a young warrior. He was in love with the beautiful princess and she was in love with him. But before they could get married, another dangerous tribe attacked their tribe. The leader of Popocatepetl's tribe spoke to him. "We need you to help our tribe before you marry my daughter," he said. Popocatepetl had to say goodbye to Iztaccihuatl, and go and fight.

'Iztaccihuatl was lonely and sad. One day she heard that Popocatepetl was dead. She became very ill. In the end, she died of a broken heart.

'But Popocatepetl wasn't dead. Very soon, he returned. When he discovered that Iztaccihuatl was dead, he picked up her body in his arms and carried her away. He laid her down on the ground in a quiet place, and sat down next to her. Snow fell and covered their two bodies.'

The guide stopped and pointed up at the two mountains in front of them. 'Look! Popocatepetl and Iztaccihuatl are still there! They are the two volcanoes.'

3 Choose the correct sentence. Discuss your choice with a partner.

The story of Popocatepetl and Iztaccihuatl is a true story.
The story of Popocatepetl and Iztaccihuatl is a legend.

4 Play the game.

Think of a true story or a legend. Tell the story to a partner. Your partner guesses if your story is a true story or a legend.

1 Look at the pictures in Activity 2. Answer the questions.

Who's on holiday?   Where are they?

2 Read the words. Match them with picture a, b or c.

Nouns: suitcase tent boy fire rucksack parents bedroom Mum Frank eggs

Verbs: Hurry up! camp cook pack laugh talk

Adjectives: late friendly bored cloudy happy

a

b

c

Picture a: bedroom, hurry up!, pack …

3 Choose some of the words and finish these sentences.

Picture a: Frank …

Picture b: Mum …

Picture c: When they arrived, …

In the evening …

Write between 20 and 30 words – you don't need to write more.

mission in action!

Write a review about the summer camp.

My mission diary
Activity Book page 106

- Write the best thing about the summer camp.
- Write the worst thing about the summer camp.
- Present your summer camp and review.

The hiking trip was the worst. We got lost and it was frightening.

The horse-riding activity was the best. It was really amazing to see the sea from the top of the mountain.

Can you remember?

1. How did Pablo's superhero catch the strange man?
2. Whose favourite day was the trip to the funfair?
3. What did George and Katy do before their windsurfing lesson?
4. Which Diversicus character couldn't find his pyjamas?
5. Name five things you should take when you go hiking.
6. Who was Popocatepetl?

Review ● ● ● Units 7–9

1 Watch the video and do the quiz.

2 9.14 Listen to George and Helen and name the buildings on the map.

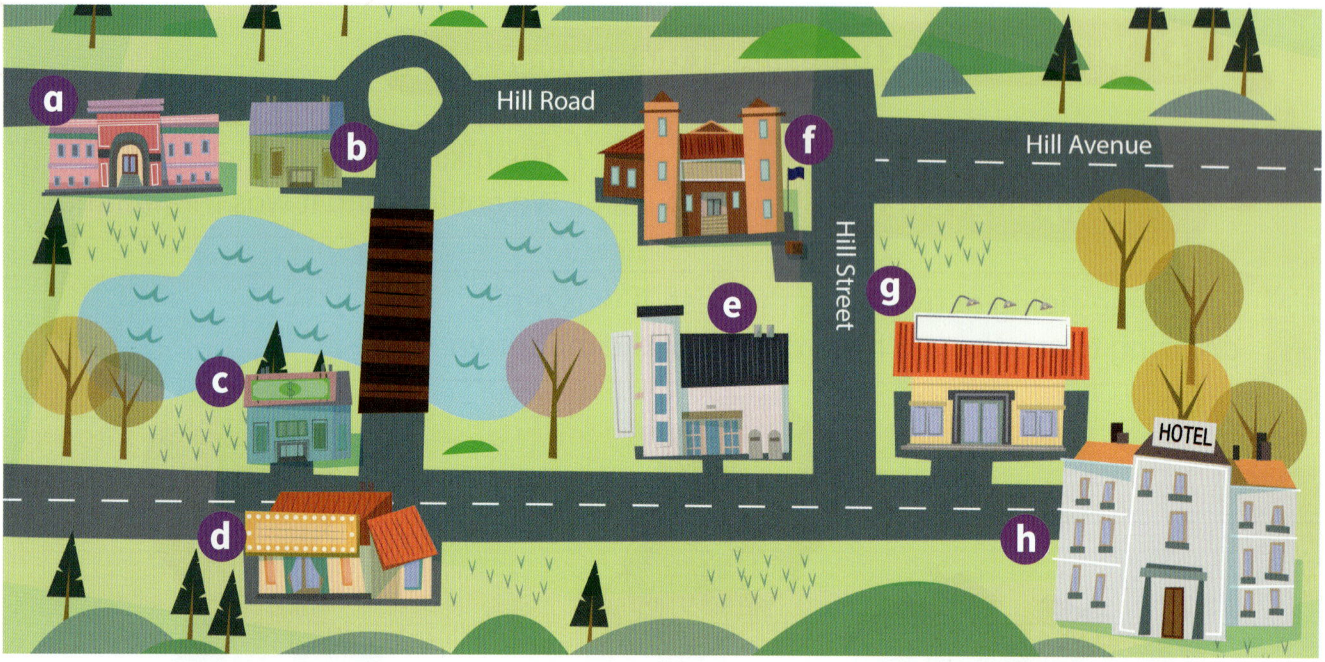

3 Work with a partner. Say which word is different and why.

1	brave	friendly	**unkind**
2	restaurant	chemist's	waiter
3	excellent	brilliant	horrible
4	pleasing	interesting	excited
5	money	post office	bank
6	driver	singer	dancer
7	tent	suitcase	hotel
8	north	straight on	east
9	huge	little	lazy
10	popular	unfriendly	lucky

Number 1. Unkind is different because brave and friendly are positive and unkind is negative.

4 Choose five words from Activity 3 to talk about people you know.

My cousin is a firefighter and she's very brave.

5 Read and complete the letter.

tour	pleased	when	bored	hotel	~~excited~~	worried
suitcase	come	worried	interesting	when		

Hi William!

How are you? I was so happy to hear from you.

I'm so [1] excited ! I'm going to go to the beach with my family tomorrow! We wanted to go camping but [2] ... my brother said he was [3] ... about sleeping in a tent, my parents said we could go to a [4] ... . My parents are [5] ... because my rucksack is packed! But they are [6] ... because my sister's [7] ... is huge!

[8] ... we arrive, we're going to go on a [9] ... of the museum. I think museums are [10] ... but my brother always feels [11] ... . He wants to build sandcastles.

Where are you going to go on your holiday? If you [12] ... to my country, please write and tell me.

Love, Nicola

6 Write a reply to Nicola.

Where am I going to go on holiday?

Who am I going to go with?

What are we going to do?

How do we feel?

Grammar reference

Unit 1

Review question words: *how, what, when, where, which, who, why*

- We use *which, how, what, when, where, who* and *why* to ask questions. We use them to get information, we don't answer with 'yes' or 'no'.

Which *acrobat is practising now?*	→	***Ivan*** *is practising now.*
How *are you today?*	→	*I'm* ***very well****, thank you.*
What *is she doing?*	→	*She's* ***having lunch****.*
When *does he have dinner?*	→	*He has dinner* ***at half past six****.*
Where *is the school?*	→	*It's* ***next to the park****.*
Why *are we getting up early today?*	→	***Because*** *school starts at seven o'clock.*
Who *are they talking to?*	→	*They're talking to* ***the teacher****.*

Remember:
I am = I'm   It is = It's   He is = He's   She is = She's
We are = We're   You are = You're   They are = They're

Was/were + could

- We use *was/were + could* to talk about an ability in the past.

I	***could***	*say a few*	***I***	***was***
She	***couldn't***	*words when*	***she***	*two.*
He			***he***	

When	*you* *we* *they*	***were*** *three,*	*you* *we* *they*	***could*** ***couldn't***	*ride a bike.*

Could	*I* *she* *he*	*play the guitar when*	*I* *she* *he*	***was***	*four?*
	you *we* *they*		*you* *we* *they*	***were***	

Yes,	*I* *she* *he* *you* *we* *they*	*could.*

No,	*I* *she* *he* *you* *we* *they*	*couldn't.*

Unit 2

Defining relative clauses

- We use defining relative clauses to give important information about something.
  - We use *who* when we are talking about **a person**.
  - We use *which* when we are talking about **a thing**.
  - We use *where* when we are talking about **a place**.

That's the	*teacher*	***who***	*I like best.*
	car	***which***	*my dad wants to buy.*
	park	***where***	*we play football.*

Remember:
That is = That's

Past simple + *when*

- We use *when* and the past simple to talk about two things that happened close together in the past.

+	***When*** *we* ***saw*** *our friends,*	→	*we* ***told*** *them about our day.*
?	***When*** *you* ***saw*** *your friends,*	→	***did you tell*** *them about your day?*
+	*We* ***told*** *our friends about our day*	→	***when*** *we* ***saw*** *them.*
?	***Did*** *you* ***tell*** *your friends about your day*	→	***when*** *you* ***saw*** *them?*
?	***What did*** *they* ***do***	→	***when*** *they* ***got*** *home yesterday?*

Remember:
(present) What does/do …? = (past) What did …?
(present) Do you …? = (past) Did you …?

Unit 3

Review of comparative and superlative adjectives, *as … as*:

- We use the **comparative** to talk about how two things compare.
  Mrs Friendly is ***taller than*** *Su-Lin.*
- We use the **superlative** to say something has more than the rest of the group.
  Ivan is ***the tallest*** *person in Diversicus.*
- Another way to make a comparison is using ***not as … as***.
  Mrs Friendly and Su-Lin ***aren't as tall as*** *Ivan.*
- We use ***as … as*** to say that two things are the same.
  Ivan is ***as tall as*** *a tree!*

Remember:
We use *-er/-est* with short adjectives, e.g. *small* = *smaller/smallest*.
We use *more/the most* with long adjectives, e.g. *dangerous* = *more/the most dangerous*.

want/need + infinitive

- We use *want* to say when we would like something. We use *need* to give advice.

I *You* *We* *They*	***want***	***to go** to the park.*
	don't want	
He	***wants***	
She	***doesn't want***	

I *You* *We* *They*	***need***	***to drink** a glass of water.*
	don't need	
He	***needs***	
She	***needs***	

Do	*I* *you* *we* *they*	***need*** ***want***	***to get** some sleep?*
Does	*she* *he*		

Remember:
do not = don't
does not = doesn't

Unit 4

Adverbs

- We use adverbs to describe how something happens or how someone does something.

	Adjective	Adverb
add *-ly*	*slow* *careful* *quiet* *quick* *bad* *loud* *beautiful*	*Walk **slowly** in the classroom.* *Listen **carefully** to the teacher.* *Work together **quietly**, please.* *Finish your lunch **quickly**.* *You don't draw **badly**!* *Don't speak **loudly**, please.* *He sings **beautifully**.*
change *-y* to *-i*, add *-ly*	*easy*	*I can do this homework **easily**.*
irregular	*good*	*You can play football very **well**!*
stay the same	*fast* *hard*	*She can run **fast**.* *Look **hard** at the sentence. Can you see the mistake?*

Comparative adverbs

- We can make comparisons of actions using adverbs. We use comparative adverbs when we want to compare how something is done.

My sister swims	***faster***	***than*** *me.*
	more quickly	

I can move more quietly than an elephant!

Be made of

- We use *be made of* to say what material something is.

It	***is***	***made of*** *wood.*
	isn't	
They	***are***	
	aren't	

Is	*it*	***made of*** *wood?*
Are	*they*	***made of*** *wood?*

Yes,	*it* ***is.***
	they ***are.***
No,	*it* ***isn't.***
	they ***aren't.***

This scarf is made of wool.

Remember:
is not = isn't
are not = aren't

shall, could and *let's* for suggestions

- We use *shall, could* and *let's* to make suggestions.

Shall	***we***	***make*** *an acrobat costume?*
	I	

We could	***use*** *card for the hats.*
Let's	***make*** *masks for the theatre workshop?*

Let's dress up like pirates! Arr!

Unit 5

Unit 6

should/*shouldn't*

- We use *should* and *shouldn't* to give advice. We use *should* to talk about things which are a good idea. We use *shouldn't* to talk about things which are a bad idea.

I *You* *He* *She* *We* *They*	***should do** the homework.*
	***shouldn't be** late for school.*

Should	*I* *you* *he* *she* *we* *they*	***go** to the beach?*

Yes,	*I* *you* *he* *she* *we* *they*	***should.***
No,		***shouldn't.***

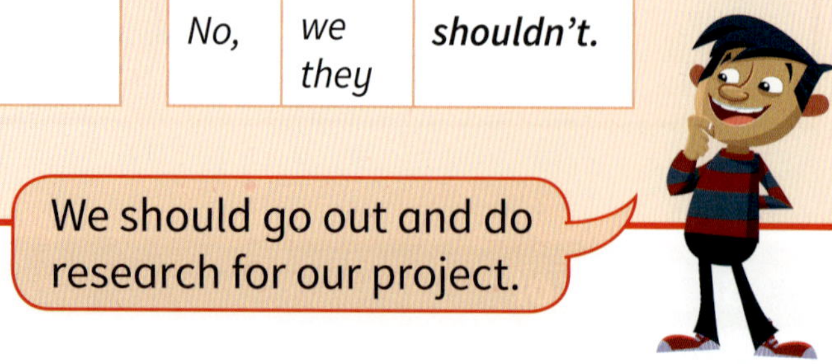

be good at + noun, *be good at* + gerund

- We use *be good at* when we want to say what subject or activity a person does well.

+	*Lily is very **good at football**.*
-	*We aren't very **good at skipping**.*
?	*Are you **good at running** and **climbing**?*
?	*What **are** they **good at**?*

Unit 7

when and *if* clauses (zero conditionals)

- We use *when* and *if* clauses to talk about results which are always true.

***if*/*when* + present simple**	**present simple**
***If** you **want** to learn to dance,*	*you **can** do classes after school.*
***When** the weather **is** cold,*	*I **wear** my warm coat.*

Present simple	***if*/*when* + present simple**
*We **don't play** football*	***if** it's **raining**.*
*Emma **does** her homework before dinner*	***when** she **gets** home early.*

look like, be like

- We use *look like* to talk about a person's physical appearance.
- We use *be like* to talk about a person's personality.

*What does your sister **look like**?*	→	*She's tall with dark hair.*
*What**'s** your sister **like**?*	→	*She's kind and friendly.*

be going to

- We use *be going to* to talk about our plans for the future. We can also use it to make predictions.

+			
I	***am***	***going to***	***go** to the cinema.*
She He	***is***		
You We They	***are***		

-			
I	***am not***	***going to***	***listen** to music.*
She He	***isn't***		
You We They	***aren't***		

?			
Is	*she he*	***going to***	***eat** dinner?*
Are	*you we they*		

+		
Yes,	*she he*	***is.***
	you we they	***are.***

-		
No,	*she he*	***isn't.***
	you we they	***aren't.***

Prepositions of movement: *across, into, out of, over, past, round, through*

- We use prepositions of movement to talk about how someone or something moves.

Henry walked	*across*	*the river.*	
Please come	*into*	*the house.*	
Turn left when you go	*out of*	*the door.*	
The bird flew	*over*	*the building.*	
Every day I go	*past*	*the bank.*	
We usually walk	*round*	*the lake.*	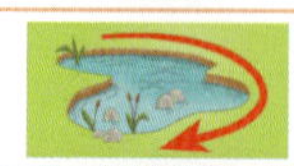
To get home, Lucy goes	*through*	*the forest.*	

Unit 9

before, after, when clauses

- We can use *before, after* and *when* clauses to talk about when two things happened. *Before* means earlier and *after* means later. We use *when* to describe events happening at the same time.

Let's go to the museum	→	***before** we eat lunch.*
Let's eat lunch	→	***after** we go to the museum.*
Let's decide what to do next	→	***when** we're eating lunch.*

–ed / *–ing* adjective endings

- We use *-ed* adjectives to talk about how we feel.
- We use *-ing* adjectives to describe a person, thing or situation.

bor-	**ing**	*This book is very **boring**.*
	ed	*I'm **bored** of reading this book.*
interest-	**ing**	*The film about Mexico was **interesting**.*
	ed	*Emily was **interested** in the film about Mexico.*
tir-	**ing**	*The walk to the waterfall was very **tiring**.*
	ed	*We were very **tired** when we arrived at the waterfall.*

Irregular verb list

Base form	Past simple
be	was
begin	began
bring	brought
build	built
buy	bought
can	could
catch	caught
choose	chose
come	came
do	did
drive	drove
eat	ate
fall	fell
feel	felt
find	found
fly	flew
forget	forgot
get	got
give	gave
go	went
grow	grew
have	had
hear	heard
hide	hid
hold	held
keep	kept

Base form	Past simple
learn	learnt
let	let
lose	lost
make	made
mean	meant
meet	met
must	had to
put	put
ride	rode
run	ran
say	said
see	saw
send	sent
sit	sat
speak	spoke
stand	stood
swim	swam
take	took
teach	taught
tell	told
think	thought
throw	threw
wake	woke
wear	wore
write	wrote

I'm a great communicator

We communicate with words, actions, pictures, songs and movement. We are communicating all the time!

1 Think and find as many words as you can related to circuses. Use a dictionary to help you. Share your words with your classmates and make a class word cloud to display them.

2 Read the following riddle. Then choose a word from the unit and create your own riddle.

I grow on trees.
I can be green or red.
I am white inside.
I am a healthy fruit.

3 As a class, create a warm-up routine for your sport class. Draw pictures to explain the exercises and add simple sentences. Share it with your P.E. teacher.

4 As a class, create vocabulary cards with new vocabulary in the unit. Keep them in a bag or a box. Every day, take turns to pick a card and describe it to your classmates. Can they guess the word?

5 In pairs, make a list of all the clothes your classmates are wearing in class today. Make a wordsearch with the words. Swap your wordsearch with another pair. Can they find all the words in two minutes?

6 Invent a short story called: *My favourite day at school.* Think of different ways to present your story to the class.

7 Create a class rap. Everyone in your class says their name and one thing about themselves using adjectives. For example, *My name's Luke and I'm friendly! I'm Maria and I'm energetic!* If the rap pauses for too long, you have to start again!

8 Create a crossword with definitions of places in town. Ask a family member to do your crossword. If they can't speak English, you can translate the definitions for them and teach them the new words.

9 Write in the air! Choose an adjective and use your fingers to write it in the air. Your classmate needs to try to guess the word. Take turns to be the air writers.

I'm multilingual

We learn different languages to communicate with others and understand different cultures.

1. Find the words in the word snake below:

DANCESHOUTLAUNCHJUMPHOPCLIMBDRESSUPSKIP

Ask a family member to help you find out the words in a different language and make a new word snake. Can your classmates guess where the new words begin and end? Are there any words that are similar in Spanish or English?

2. In groups, design menus for a restaurant. Your menu must be in English and Spanish. Include pictures to help identify the food. Are any words the same or similar in both languages?

3. Find five examples of basketball teams around the world which include an animal in the name. Draw the logos.

4. Symbols help us identify things without words. Look at a physical map and find examples of symbols. How do you say these things in your language? Make a poster with all the symbols you found as a class. Write the words in Spanish and in English underneath.

5 Some names of clothes are the same or very similar in lots of different languages. Can you find some examples?

6 Imagine you are at school in a different country. Translate your weekly timetable into the language they speak in that country. Are there any school subjects that sound funny in the other language? Do you think any sound better than in your language?

7 The word *doctor* is used in lots of languages. Can you find some examples? Where did this word come from originally and what did it mean in the past? Investigate!

8 In groups, find out how to say *school* in ten different languages. Make a word cloud on a piece of paper. Display it in the classroom.

9 Put a map of Europe on the wall in your classroom. Find out how to say *Have a good journey!* in different European languages. As a class, add the phrases to the map next to each country. Choose where you want to go on holiday. Your classmates can wish you a happy holiday in the correct language: *Have a good journey!*

I'm a STEM expert

We experiment and learn from our mistakes. We are inventive and full of questions!

1. Look at the chart with the prices. How much is it for your family to go to the circus on a Thursday afternoon?

CIRCUS TICKETS	ADULT +18 YEARS	KIDS 2–18 YEARS	BABIES 0–2 YEARS
MONDAY TO FRIDAY	5€	3€	FREE
SATURDAY AND SUNDAY	7€	5€	FREE

2. Look at some food labels at home. What information can you find? Why is it important to know this information?

3. What do you know about bones? Read, investigate and say if the following sentences are TRUE or FALSE.

- There are 100 bones in the human body.
- The biggest bone in our head is the skull.
- When we get bigger and taller our bones grow.
- The longest bone in your body is the humerus.
- There are small bones in our ears.

4. Find out more about unusual plants around the world. Draw a picture and label the different parts of the plant. Make a crazy jungle mural in class with all the unusual plants.

5. What can you use a plastic bottle for? Find as many uses as you can as a class. Choose one of the options. Make an example over the weekend with help from a family member.

6. In pairs, look at your school timetable and ask questions about time. Here are some examples:

When do you have English?

What time do you have sport?

What time does breaktime end?

7. Find out what tools archeologists use and what they use them for. Find pictures on the internet and make an archeological dig model.

8. Investigate different tools to help us find our way. Which ones use technology? Learn how to use a compass to find north.

9. Let's pack your bags for your holiday! Is it hot or cold or something in the middle where you are going? Think and complete this diagram so you can pack a bag for all weather!

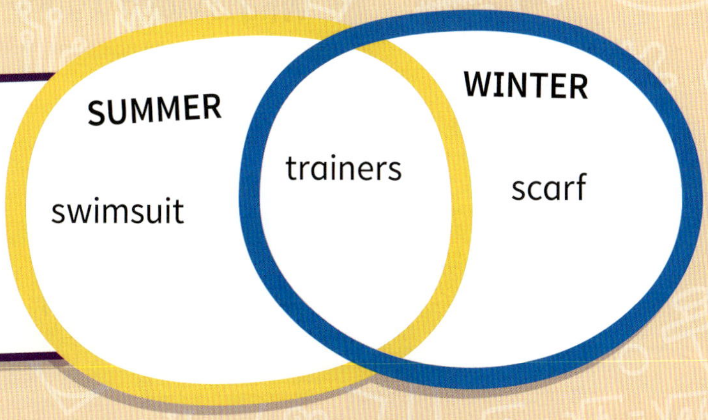

I'm a digital whizz kid

We are digital natives and we love learning with new tools. We live with technology and use it every day. We have to use it responsibly.

1. With the help of a family member, use a computer or tablet to create your own ticket to an event. It must include:
   - The date
   - The time
   - The price

2. Observe how barcodes are used in supermarkets. In some supermarkets, you can scan your own shopping. Do you do this? Think of two other places where we use barcodes. Bring some examples to show the class.

3. Learn how to juggle. Ask a family member to find a good video on the internet to help you practise. Why is video a good way to learn new things?

4. Ask a family member to help you take some close-up photos of nature with a camera phone. Investigate the special effects you can use to change your photos. Learn how to give your new photos a name and save them.

5 Find five facts on the internet about gold. Write them down and add one fact that isn't true. In class, read out your sentences and see if your classmates can guess the incorrect sentence.

Not everything on the internet is true. It is easy to invent things. What can we do to make sure we get the correct facts when we study?

6 What are you good at? Record a video of yourself talking about things you and your family are good at. Then share it with your class.

7 What is an avatar? Do you use them in class? Design an avatar to represent you and your family members.

8 Ask a family member to show you how online maps work. Get directions from your house to your school. How far is it in kilometres? How long does it take to walk? Can you use public transport to get there?

9 Use photos of your last summer holiday to create a digital story. Add speech bubbles to the photos and write funny dialogues.

I'm a super study star

We are organised, collaborative, creative and resilient pupils.

1. We learn from our mistakes. When we get something wrong, we try again. Help create a class English mistakes wall. Add common mistakes to the wall and the correction. Use colours and pictures to help you and your classmates remember the correction.

2. Investigate the Healthy Eating Plate idea. You can use it to design balanced and healthy meals. Work in groups to design a healthy meal you like.

3. When you finish a page of your English unit, invent a quiz question to help you and your classmates remember what you are learning. Add your questions to a class quiz box. Your teacher can use the questions to play games and revise language.

4. How many animals do you know as a class? In teams, take turns to write the name of an animal on a piece of paper. Read your list to the rest of the class. How many do you know together?

5 Play *I spy* in pairs to describe objects you can see in your class. Use clothes and adjectives from the unit. Say *I spy with my little eye something beginning with …* for your partner to guess the word.

6 As a class, create picture dictionary posters for each unit of your English book.

7 *When I grow up I want to be …* In groups, mime what you want to be and see if your classmates can guess the job.

8 Create a board game to use directions. Here are some ideas:

Go 1 square left.

Go through the secret door.

Go over the bridge.

Turn back 2 squares.

9 Let's play a memory game in groups! Choose a letter. You have one minute to complete the categories with words beginning with your letter.

PLACE	FOOD	THINGS	ADJECTIVE	ACTIVITY
Canada	carrot	car	cute	cooking

I'm a model citizen

We are respectful, caring and collaborative.

1. Read two examples of rules at a public event. Add more as a class. Are any of these rules good rules for school, too?
   - Don't use your mobile phone.
   - Don't drop litter.

2. Think of an example of when someone made a choice you disagreed with. How did you react? Share your example with the class and listen to your classmates' examples. What can we do to show respect for other people's choices?

3. Doctors and nurses take care of people every day. Write a letter to the nearest medical centre thanking them for their work. Draw some pictures to make them happy.

4. Find out about all the wildlife protection ideas in your local area. As a class, vote for one of these initiatives and think of ways you can contribute as a class.

5 Plastic is a very useful material we use every day, but it can be harmful to our environment. With your family, think about how to reduce plastic at home.

6 Being a good classmate is very important. Make a list of the things you should or shouldn't do when you work in groups.

7 All jobs are important. Think of five different jobs and explain why they are important.

8 Is there anything you would like to improve in your town or city? Decide as a group the most important things to change. Who can make these changes? Think of ways to communicate your ideas to the people who can make the changes.

9 Imagine a new classmate has arrived from a different country. They probably think everything seems very strange and new. What can you do to make new classmates feel welcome?

I'm a creative thinker

We solve problems creatively and share new ideas.

1. Your class has been asked to prepare a special party at school. Organise different groups to focus on different parts of the party. Listen to all the ideas as a class. Think of the best way to present the party idea to your head teacher.

2. Invent an international dinner menu with your family. Choose some meals from different countries to try each week.

3. Prepare a yoga class to do at home with your family. You can include a warm up activity, a routine and some stretching exercises.

4. Plan a class or school plant nursery. What materials do you need? How much space do you need? Where is the best place to do this in the school? Show your plan to your head teacher.

5 You want to organise a school play but you do not have money to buy costumes and props. In groups, choose a play and plan how you can make the costumes and props yourselves.

6 Help your teacher plan a school trip. What things do you have to plan?

7 Think of classroom jobs. Help create a job rota, so you and your classmates can share the jobs.

8 New pupils find it difficult to find their way around school in the first few weeks. Invent a welcome pack for new pupils. This includes a fun map to help them remember their way around the school.

9 What do you need to travel safely and comfortably? Create a recipe for travelling. You should include the ingredients and steps to follow.

I'm a cultural ambassador

We learn from other cultures and reflect on our own culture.

1. Look at pictures of special events from around the world. What can you see? What do the people do, eat and wear on the special day?

2. Investigate. Copy and complete the chart with typical meals from around the world. Here are some example countries. Would you like to try any of these recipes at home?

COUNTRY	TYPICAL MEAL
United States	
Japan	
Morocco	
Italy	
Mexico	

3. As a class, investigate typical school snacks from around the world. Are they healthy snacks? Are they similar or different to the snacks you bring to school? Make a *snack map* for the classroom showing the results of your investigation.

4. Choose a country. With the help of a family member, investigate national parks in that country and choose one. Create a classroom presentation to tell your classmates what you discovered. Find all the places your class presents on a physical map.